ARCHITECTURE

From Its Origins to the Present Day

By CHARLES RAMBERT

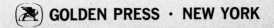

GOLDEN PRESS · NEW YORK

contents

Cover picture:
Maison de la Radio, Paris

Published in 1969 by Golden Press, New York, N.Y.,
a division of Western Publishing Company, Inc.
© Copyright 1968 by Editions des Deux Coqs d'Or, Paris,
and Mondadori-OGAM, Verona.
Library of Congress Catalog Card Number: 69–19126

terminology | 1

FRAMEWORK

The framework, whether of wood, metal, reinforced and now prestressed concrete, is the basic structure of a building. It consists of the foundations fitted to supports and connected by stringers, columns, beams, floor slabs, staircases and in certain cases vaults and wind bracing.

The framework is completed by filling and trimming. The filling may be heavy, of masonry, brick or cement block sheathed on the outside with stone slabs or covered with ceramic tile or facade panels;

or it may be light and consist of curtain walls, usually of metal and glass.

Framing systems are identified by their forms. They include the orthogonal systems (pillars and beams of skyscrapers), portal frames, arches, and reticulated and tridimensional systems formed of the assembly of a great number of bars.

The most recent framing systems consist of shells or warped surfaces and tridimensional structures which belong to space structures. These include, in addition to trusses and shells, folded plate structures and cables or mesh-supported structures which are sometimes also called suspended roofs and pretensioned shells.

Metal framework of a new building for the Family Allowances Fund in Paris. This type of framework consists of nine floors of symmetrical portal frames, using two pillars and consoles.

wooden framing

For a period of centuries, at least in Northern Europe, houses used wooden framing. This consisted of a stringer low wall plate (below, 1), resting on a masonry foundation and supporting upright posts and studs (2), which are fastened to an upper wall plate (3) supporting the ceiling joists (4). Diagonal (5) and Saint Andrew's trusses served as wind bracing. The space between the wood was filled with brick or rubble covered with a layer of plaster or stucco.

Typical of such wooden-framed houses are those built in Rouen during the first half of the 15th century. Wooden framing led naturally to the use of metal framing in the 19th century and subsequently to reinforced concrete framing in the 20th century.

Wooden framework. This building in Rouen is typical of Gothic housing techniques.

Wood is again finding structural use in the form of laminates, a technique invented by Otto Hetzer in 1906. This method consists of fabricating long spans and usually curved beams by means of clamping and gluing together 1-inch boards. The glue's strength, which is greater than that of the wood itself, and its perfect adhesion, make it possible to reconstitute rigid and immensely strong wooden beams capable of spanning 325 feet or more.

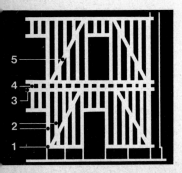

metal framing

Cast iron. Iron ore was first smelted in a blast furnace by the Englishman Darby in 1710; the first structure using this material was the 98-foot span Coalbrookdale Bridge over the Severn River, in Great Britain, built in 1779. This was followed by Paris' Pont des Arts (1803) and Pont d'Austerlitz (1806) and afterward by the pillars and arches of the Saint Geneviève Library in 1843.

Iron. Already used as a binding material in the masonry of antique temples and in a few 17th and 18th century buildings, iron became a building material in its own right thanks to metallurgical discoveries made in England in the 18th century. Paxton used iron and glass exclusively for his Crystal Palace at the 1851 London Universal

Glued laminated framing is frequently used for sports facilities such as this gymnasium near Rouen.

Exposition, and between 1854 and 1856 Paris' Les Halles were rebuilt with cast iron and iron. Between 1860 and 1871 Baltard, creator of Les Halles, built the church of Saint Augustin whose framework was also of cast iron and iron. In Paris' Gare du Nord (1863), Hittorf showed how iron could be used for a vast utilitarian building.

The first *prefabricated* building using iron framing and cast iron panels was erected by Peter Ellis in Liverpool in 1864 (Oriel Chambers, p. 8), and in the following year Giuseppe Mengoni built the soaring Victor Emmanuel Gallery in Milan, whose main entrance is as high as the nave of that city's cathedral.

7

For the 1889 Paris Universal Exposition, Dutert and Condamine threw a 351-foot span over the Gallery of Machines and Gustave Eiffel erected the famous 984-ft. tower.

From this there evolved the idea of building extremely tall structures, and the Chicago school began to erect the skyscrapers described by Louis Sullivan as "buildings rising story by story."

Steel. The United States became the champion in the use of this material, chiefly with the 1,447-foot Empire State Building (1931).

First masked behind neoclassical facades, steel framing soon became more refined, offering new forms of expression and avoidance of the architectural frauds so common in some faddish periods.

Sainte-Geneviève Library, Paris (1843). One of the first buildings to use metal framing, with cast-iron pillars and an iron vault.

Oriel Chambers, Liverpool (1864). The metal frame of this office building was covered with prefabricated cast-iron sheathing.

8

reinforced concrete and prestressed concrete

As the use of metal became popular in building, Vicat's advances in cement in 1820 opened up new vistas.

Reinforced concrete. The earliest building of reinforced concrete was erected by François Coignet in Saint Denis in 1855. In 1884 François Hennebique made the first concrete slab using round steel bars; he subsequently put up the first building with reinforced concrete, at 1 rue Danton, Paris.

Apartment house, 25 bis, rue Franklin, Paris (1903). One of the first apartment buildings to use a visible reinforced concrete framework.

The Perret brothers then decided to employ reinforced concrete "architecturally" and succeeded magnificently with their apartment house at 25 bis, rue Franklin, Paris, in 1903, and in 1905 with their rue de Ponthieu garage.

The technique seemed new yet actually represented a return to former styles, since in the Middle Ages empty space predominated over solid structure, thus making architecture a spectacular science in which decoration took second place to structure. Reinforced concrete frameworks so typical of building techniques in the first half of the 20th century quickly became standard all over the world. The most striking example is the Teikoku, or Imperial Hotel, built in Tokyo in 1916–1922 by Frank Lloyd Wright.

Prestressed concrete. Faced with stiffer competition from steel, reinforced concrete construction took a new lease on life thanks to the discovery of the technique of prestressing. This consists of reinforcing concrete with strongly stretched steel cables. This compresses the concrete and endows it with exceptional qualities of strength and elasticity—a principle demonstrated as

Marseilles, Le Corbusier's Radiant City (1947). One of the first post-war experiments in constructing a unified residential complex in a single building. It contains 1,600 dwelling units.

early as 1888 by C. E. W. Doehring, though it was not until 1928 that a French engineer, Freyssinet, perfected its applications. Prestressed concrete made possible the building of such public works as the Oléron viaduct and the Maine-Montparnasse mail-sorting centre (p. 14) in France, and in Honduras the Omonita Bridge whose main span covers 394 feet.

Mixed framing. Steel and reinforced concrete can be used in the same framework and some buildings (Paris' Maison de la Radio—p. 24) may have some parts in steel and others in reinforced concrete.

Plastic framing. Experiments have been made with plastic framing using fiberglass reinforced polyesters.

Prefabrication of components. The use of standardised framing dimensions permits the prefabrication of many structural members which, in multi-unit structures, can result in true industrialisation of building techniques.

Oléron Viaduct, a spectacular example of the use of prestressed arches. Its length is 6.2 miles.

thin shell and tridimensional structures

These forms are also known as spatial structures and include spatial trellises, folded structures, shells and structures using cables or nets, which are frequently called suspended structures or prestressed veils.

Space trusses may exist in either steel or concrete. One of the earliest uses of this technique was the market of Frankfurt-am-Main, built in 1927. This was followed by Pier Luigi Nervi's remarkable aircraft hangars with spans of 130 feet or more which employed prefabricated reinforced concrete elements. More recent applications include the sheet aluminum domes of the American architect Buckminster Fuller, the best examples of which are Paris' Palais des Sports and the great U.S. pavilion at Montreal's Expo 67 Fair. Emulating the ancients, ways are sought to eliminate costly formwork, and some of the new trussed cupolas can be erected with an inflatable balloon.

Folded plate structures. Folding gives relatively thin reinforced concrete slabs great rigidity, a structural technique resulting in completely new spatial expression, such as Pier L. Nervi's meeting hall at the Paris UNESCO and Gillet, Lafaille and Sarger's church of Notre-Dame de Royan (p. 218–219).

Shells. These are apt to be thin in spite of the great spans involved. The thickness/span ratio was 1/33 for Saint

U.S. Pavilion at Expo 67, Montreal. Its immense geodesic dome is a fine application of the latest space techniques.

Peter's in Rome, but only 1/666 for the Zeiss planetarium in Jena and a startling 1/1570 for the C.N.I.T. exhibition building at Paris's Rond Point de la Défense.

Shell segments. Curved in the direction of the span, they permit spans of 984 feet for a thickness of only 4 inches. The C.N.I.T. building, which covers an equilateral triangle 705 feet on each side, consists of shell segments joined to form a triple-fanned dome (p. 235, far right).

UNESCO, Paris. Folded plate construction is used for the rear of this conference hall by Pier Luigi Nervi.

Two examples of thin shells. The M.I.T. auditorium in Cambridge, Mass. (1) rests on three supports, while the Royan market, France (2), uses a conoid system.

Little Sports Palace, Rome (1957). A shell buttressed by Y-shaped pillars according to a technique perfected by Pier Luigi Nervi.

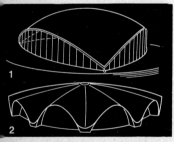

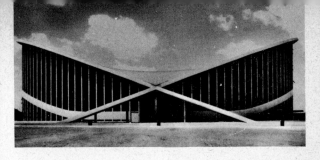

As an example of a large volume enclosed by three-sided segments cut from a flattened dome, we might cite Saarinen's auditorium for the Massachusetts Institute of Technology in Cambridge.

Cylindrical shells are seen in huge cantilevers such as the Hanover stadium in Germany and the Cartagena stadium in Colombia. The intersections of the shells at the St. Louis, Missouri, airport are reminiscent of groined vaults.

Shells of revolution are most widespread of all. Pier Luigi Nervi's Rome Sports Palace is a remarkable example.

Hyperboloid sections. Mexican architect Felix Candela specialises in this form of shell, sometimes known as the saddleback shell. In Europe, Le Corbusier provided an outstanding example in his Philips pavilion for the Brussels World's Fair of 1958.

The Raleigh Arena, N.C. An application of roofing systems using pretensioned reverse curvature cables.

Free form. Sarger's Royan market in France and Saarinen's TWA terminal at Kennedy Airport, New York, are notable free-form structures.

The present trend is toward cable and mesh construction, the principles of which were long applied to suspension bridges. These may be divided into different categories such as single curvature suspended roofs, as in the Wuppertal swimming pool in Germany; a reverse curvature cable mesh whose rigidity is obtained by pretensioning, as in the Raleigh, N.C., stadium; combined structures using cables and bars like the U.S. pavilion at the Brussels Fair of 1958, and tensioned roofs such as the one covering the Yale hockey stadium in New Haven.

13

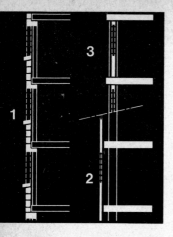

walls

Bearing walls. In traditional construction, the wall is a masonry structure whose thickness may vary from 8 inches to 24½ feet (Coucy Castle, France) and consisting of layers of material bound together with lime mortar, plaster, cement or even mud.

Sustaining walls (1) may be either homogeneous, entirely of cut stone, or built with foundations and bond-beams of stone with brick filling (Louis XIII style). The way in which materials are cut and arranged is called the *bond*.

Cross-walls, perpendicular to the facade, are intended to reduce the span and help support the floors and roof framing. *Cable walls* are used on each end of a building and may either project above the roof line or be covered by the roof. *Facade walls* are topped by entablatures derived from the antique or by cornices.

Non-bearing walls. In this case, walls become nothing more than a filling between the uprights of the framing (3). When the facing is outside of the framing it is known as a curtain wall (2), and the sheathing, usually about 2 inches thick, shows an independent pattern. A good example is the Nobel Tower in Puteaux, France.

Comparative sections of a traditional bearing, or sustaining, wall (1, left) and framework construction (3, 2, right).

Maine-Montparnasse mail-sorting centre, Paris. It is one part of a complex in which prestressed elements were widely used.

arches

An arch is a curved stone structure whose two ends are supported by pillars or uprights. The stones or keys are shaped in such a manner that their joints converge, thus distributing the load to the supports.

Arches, which eventually resulted in vaults, were a great advance over the post and lintel construction of the Greeks and Egyptians. They formed one of the basic elements of Roman architecture and an essential technique of the Middle Ages, particularly the Gothic period.

There are several forms of arches: semi-circular, flattened, broken, etc., which may vary according to different periods, countries and styles. A succession of arches forms either a barrel vault (Vézelay, p. 97) or an arcade (Foundling Hospital, Florence, p. 134).

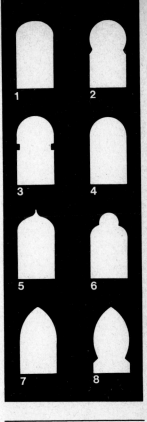

Eight types of arches:

1 flattened	5 bracketed
2 horseshoe	6 trilobed
3 broken	7 Gothic (ogival)
4 semicircular	8 lanceolate

The principle of the arch, showing the direction of the thrust and the keystone at top of the vault.

vaults

Vaults are a structural system of Sumerian origin and consist of rings of bricks or stones resting against each other to form a curve, the purpose being to augment the size of rooms. Previously room sizes had been limited to the possibilities offered by the use of posts, lintels and stone slabs.

The difference is particularly noticeable if we compare the plan of an Egyptian hypostyle hall, which was covered with stone slabs resting on a forest of close-set, cumbersome columns (the propylaea of Karnak, 1), with that of a Roman bath with its vast rooms free of inner supports (as in the case of the baths of Agrippa, 2).

Actually, necessity was the mother of invention in this case, for brick vaults came into being because there was no wood for construction in the arid plains of the Middle East far from the coast. Thus the first brick domes appeared near Hama in Syria, while the first Egyptian vaults were made of brick rings of decreasing diameter in Abydos (3).

Barrel vaults were typical of antique vaults and remained popular in Egypt and Assyria. Strabo reports that they were built in vertical sections and without falsework, since there was no wood. The great halls of Assyrian palaces

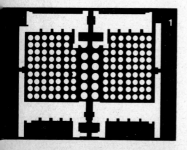

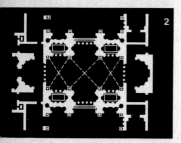

used barrel vaults. The simplest and most widespread type of barrel vault is an extended arch whose stones are called *voussoirs* (the church at Saint-Savin-sur-Gartempe, for instance), and this type of vault remained popular in architectural practice throughout the Romanesque period.

Depending on their alignment, barrel vaults can be considered semi-circular, flattened or broken. Barrel vaults are sometimes strengthened by projecting arches known as transverse arches, as may be seen in the church of Sainte Madeleine at Vézelay (p. 97).

Groined vaults. The intersection at right angles of two barrel vaults of the same height forms ridges or groins.

This type of vaulting was favored by the Romans (the basilica of Constantine and the baths of Diocletian). It developed rapidly during the Middle Ages due to the crossed ogives whose origins can be found in ribbed vaults (and, above all, domes) used in architecture in Russian Georgia, Spain, Morocco and Armenia during the 9th and 10th centuries.

Durham Cathedral, England, started in 1094, provides the finest example of the transition between groin vaults and ribbed vaults. This was followed in France by an extraordinary succession of vaults culminating in the crossed ogives of the 13th century.

Crossed ogives (1). These vaults are built on ribs or ogives which cross at right angles and diagonally, and have broken arches fore and

Structure of a groined vault showing ribs and filling.

Principle of a barrel vault, showing transverse arch.

aft and wall arches along the sides. The ribs, of which there are usually four (quadripartite vault), may be increased to make sexpartite or octopartite vaults or fan vaults by using liernes and tiercerons. Such vaults are the basis of Gothic construction, of which Chartres Cathedral is perhaps the most beautiful example.

Like groin vaults, crossed ogives distribute the downward stress to the supports, but they are both lighter and stronger and are better able to withstand warping. Crossed ogives quickly replaced all other types of vaults.

Intersecting barrel vaults (2). Classic and Baroque architects abandoned the Gothic vaulting system in favor of barrel vaults in new shapes: deeply penetrating lateral vaults, intersecting vaults whose tops were not on the same level (the refectory of the Abbaye aux Hommes, or Men's Abbey, in Caen, rebuilt during the 18th century) and basket-handle vaults.

Square domes (3). Used to cover square rooms, these vaults were in fact domes built in four equal sections (Palatine Chapel, Aix-la-Chapelle).

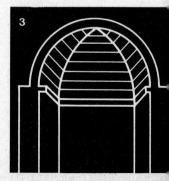

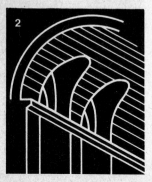

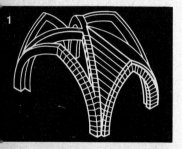

domes

Vaults in the form of a hemisphere are ideal to roof round buildings. Nevertheless, they may also be used to cover square buildings, in which case two methods are used to square the circle. *Squinches* (1) convert the square into an octagon as in Notre Dame des Doms in Avignon, while *pendentives* (2), or concave triangles, join the square to the circle, as may be seen in Istanbul's Santa Sophia.

The best example of a stone dome is that of the Pantheon in Rome.

Domes again became popular after the Gothic sway had

The dome of Saint Peter's, Rome. This brilliantly constructed dome marks the apogee of the Italian Renaissance. Its diameter is 135 feet.

lost ground. Renaissance architects drew their inspiration from Santa Sophia's immense 98-foot dome, going on to build domes over the Cathedral of Santa Maria del Fiore in Florence and then Saint Peter's in Rome, where the great dome is 135 feet in diameter.

During the classical period the inner dome was covered with a masonry or framed sheathing to raise it still higher. Typical of this type of construction are the domes of the Invalides in Paris and Saint Paul's in London.

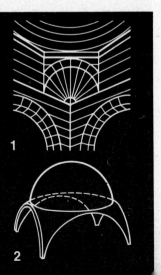

openings

Openings, doors and windows are characterised by their overall proportions and the design of their component parts. The lower parts consist of a threshhold (for a door) or sill (for a window). On each side are uprights, jambs or jamb linings whose tops are sometimes enlarged by crossettes. At the upper end is a lintel (1), which may be topped by a stress-relieving arch (2) or a flat arch of masonry (3), supplemented by a crown or arch.

The crown is sometimes supported by consoles, thus extending the top of the frame to create a triangular or curved *pediment*. During classical periods, columns or pilasters were often used on either side of the openings.

While the keystone (4) is the basic part of an arch, the support is also important in that its carefully designed profile includes a groove known as a drip which protects the walls and the window basements from rain.

Windows have grown steadily in size. Their alignment changed from vertical to horizontal in the 20th century.

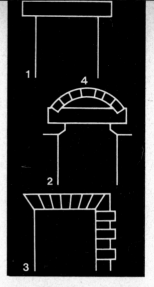

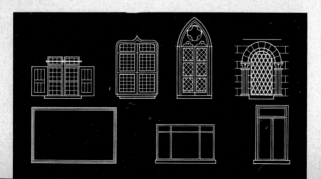

roof framing

Roof framing consists essentially of trusses made of wood (1), metal or concrete.

A truss is a rigid assembly which generally assumes the form of an isoceles triangle. The different parts of a truss are the tie beam at the bottom, the main rafters and a vertical element, the king post. Trusses are connected to one another by purlins—wall plate purlin, intermediary purlin and ridge-pole, and by diagonal braces.

Inclined sky beams (2) are also used, either to diminish the useless space under the rafters or to create an attic or living space. The idea of living under the rafters led to the Mansart roof (3).

The shape of roofs is perhaps more a matter of ethnic choice rather than of climatic necessity. Only thus can we explain high-rising Chinese and Japanese roofs, whose structural system is entirely different, since the truss principle is ignored (4) and only superimposed portal frames are used. Ethnic choice perhaps also explains the odd shapes of Russian "bulbs" and the French and British love of domes, e.g., the Invalides (5).

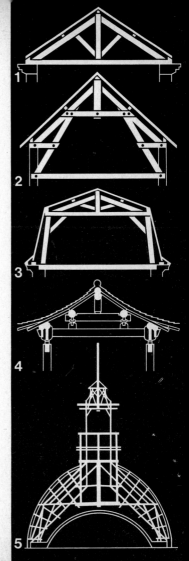

roofs

The purpose of a roof is to shelter a building from the weather. It usually consists of a framework covered with any number of watertight materials. Since the beginning of architecture, almost every conceivable material has been employed.

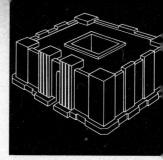

The roof's slope generally determines which material is to be utilised; slate, for example, is the usual choice for steep roofs. One of the most important parts of a roof is the valley-channel where two slopes meet.

While tall, steep roofs are efficient in cold rainy climates, terraces are indicated where the weather is warm and dry. Thus there has been a geographical differentiation in roof styles over the centuries, but even this has disappeared apparently, now that watertight techniques have been perfected, and terraced roofs have become increasingly popular.

Though terraced roofs are representative of the Mediterranean basin, they were not used exclusively. In Italy and southern France buildings are generally topped by gently sloped tile roofs—in contrast to northern France, Belgium and Germany where steep-sloped slate roofs are the rule. Since Gothic days the battle between Mediterranean and Northern influences has raged unabated, with the

---

General roofing terminology

1 eave	7 roof tree
2 hip rafter	8 flat roof
3 break	9 overhang
4 slope	10 valley channel
5 hip or ridge	11 cutter
6 break line	12 dormer

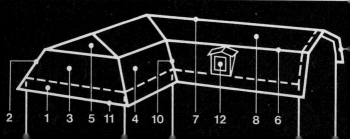

2 1 3 5 11 4 10 7 12 8 6

Château de Saint-Germain-en-Laye. Terraced roofs, typical of the Mediterranean area, were also adopted by the antique-inspired French Renaissance.

Left (top), a typical Sumerian terrace.
Right, high-rising Japanese roofs: the castle of Osaka (1587).

victory going first to one style and then to the other.

For instance, the French Renaissance, with its passion for things antique, opted for terraces and loggias like those at Saint-Germain-en-Laye. Yet in many cases, architects wishing to give an impression of a terrace actually built terraced roofs consisting of very slightly sloped roofs hidden behind an acroterium or balustrade (colonnade of the Louvre and the garden facade of Versailles).

The two techniques are sometimes combined. The Louis XIII parts of Versailles have slate sections while the Louis XIV parts are terraced. The chapel is the only exception, and its steeply sloped slate roof recalls the medieval tradition.

A return to Antique styles usually results in a recrudescence of terraces—witness the Renaissance under François I, the early days of Louis XIV, and the latter half of the 18th century in France.

new materials

The development of steel and concrete as building materials led to a new form of architecture based on independent frame buildings, and this in turn made the use of new materials necessary.

Glass. Though glass is not a new material as such, many interesting applications of it have appeared recently: thick glass; composite glazing using a sandwich construction with either air or a third pane as a filler; insulating glass;

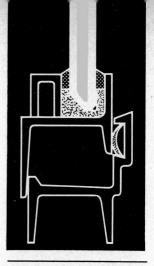

Insulating glass, consisting of two panes with a vacuum in between, is ideal for buildings with extensive window space.

Maison de la Radio, Paris. Modern materials were used throughout, particularly for the curtain walls, which are made of light alloys.

glass bricks and floor tile; heating glass, and fiberglas as insulation.

Insulation has become one of the architect's major concerns because of new heating techniques, such as electricity, which are costly; and because of increased window space, the use of extremely thin curtain walls and the reduction of space between ceiling and roof.

Light alloys. Aluminum was isolated as an element in 1827 by a German, Wöhler, and produced industrially for the first time in 1854 by Sainte-Claire Deville. Light alloys based on aluminum make it possible to produce light, slightly sloped roofs (self-supporting trays), facade sheathing in the form of curtain walls (see p. 14), metal window framing and adjustable interior partitions. Paris' Maison de la Radio made great use of light alloys, particularly as a surfacing material.

Plastics. The result of Baekeland's pioneering work of 1909 is the almost unlimited application of plastics: as structural elements, floor and wall covering, pipe, plumbing fixtures, roofing elements, insulation and paint. Polyester, polyvinyl chloride (PVC), acrylic resins, expanded polystyrene, polyurethane foam and silicones are all employed. To show what could be done, the Charbonnages de France (the nationalised coal-mining system) built an all-plastic house in 1956 (see p. 25).

stairways

Many ways of getting from one level to another have developed in the course of the ages.

Straight stairways. These were widespread in ancient Eastern civilisations (ziggurat of Ur),

A demonstration of the use of synthetic materials in architecture: the all-plastic house designed and built by the Charbonnages de France.

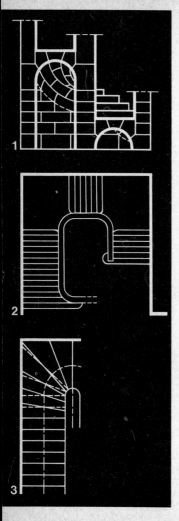

1

2

3

in Greek architecture (the propylaea), among the Mayans (pyramid and temple of Chichén-Itzá) and in China (temple of T'ai Ho Tien).

Spiral staircases. Built as a spiral corbelled vault (1), this type of staircase abounded during the Middle Ages (Coucy Castle) and then during the Renaissance, when fresher and more graceful forms were developed (Anet, Chambord, Blois and Montal castles).

French-style staircases (2) consist of three ramps and two landings placed in a rectangle or square, as at the Hôtel Peyrenc de Moras (p. 180) in Paris or in the Petit Trianon at Versailles.

Straight or quarter-turn ramps are usually built on stringers or racks, while stone staircases, and particularly outside ones, derive their support from string walls.

The most important concept in a quarter-turn ramp is its balance (3) and the fact that the width of the steps decreases toward the railing.

types of plans

Buildings can be distinguished by their floor plan, volume, facade and style. We could almost say that the character of a building depends above all on its *floor plan*.

Symmetrical and asymmetrical plans. Irregular floor plans have been opposed to symmetrical plans throughout the ages, and a comparison is frequently drawn between the civil architecture of the Gothic period and that built during the classic epoch. Nevertheless, when a building is enlarged over a period of years, both symmetrical and asymmetrical elements may be included. The palace of Fontainebleau is an example.

Square or rectangular plans, with an inner courtyard, are typical of the entire Mediterranean basin, except for ancient Crete. Rectangular buildings are especially suitable when monumental effects are sought.

The basilical plan originated in Rome with nave, transept and apse. Basic to Christian architecture, it was widely used for Romanesque and Gothic cathedrals (1).

Central plans are inscribed in a circle or square (2), and include all round and octagonal buildings as well as those using a Greek cross where the two axes are equal, as in the Church of the Holy Sepulchre in Jerusalem or the Panthéon in Paris. Many variations are possible, including tall modern apartment houses which often have a star-shaped plan (3).

Ring plans, recalling the Colosseum, occasionally with a central tower, have become popular in the 20th century as have *serpentine plans* which can take full advantage of sunshine and landscaped settings (Brasília).

1   2   3

THE BIRTH OF ARCHITECTURE

Prehistory. One of man's first concerns was to find shelter, and nature helped him in this respect by providing caves such as those at Altamira or Lascaux. However, as rocky terrain was not always available, man was forced to build shelters such as huts and cabins.

Early civilisations. Yet the first civilisations had to emerge in order for us to speak of true architecture. It was then that the first designed houses appeared with more than just simple sleeping quarters—the first habitable space.

The Iranian plateau seems to have been the cradle of Western civilisation. In ancient Babylonia, near the Persian Gulf, Sumerian art blossomed between the years 3500 and 2000 B.C.—at the same time that the Pharaohs extended their reign over all Egypt.

Other cultures also dawned: the Chinese in the Yellow River valley and the Indian along the banks of the Indus. In America, successive migrations flowed over the continent from Asia, about 25,000 B.C.

Stonehenge, England, stone circle of the early Bronze Age. Megaliths can be considered one of the earliest forms of architecture.

SUMER, ASSYRIA, PERSIA

Wood and stone being scarce in Mesopotamia, that fertile land between the Tigris and the Euphrates, buildings were made of unbaked brick covered often with a protective layer of mud. The use of such material necessitated very thick walls with narrow windows and doors.

Sumer

Back in the 24th century B.C., this region enjoyed a valid architecture, with city planning which included whole blocks of buildings around the royal palace and temple-topped ziggurat. Typical of Sumerian architecture was the almost ubiquitous use of the vault.

Ziggurat. The first stepped tower, atop which the deity was said to reside, appeared in Uruk. It became the prototype for many other similar terraced edifices which

The ziggurat of Ur. Atop this stepped brick tower, the divinity resided in a small temple.

for a thousand years dotted the Mesopotamian landscape. One of these, seven stories tall with a height of almost 300 feet, achieved later fame from its biblical description as the Tower of Babel (a name derived from the Hebrew word for Babylonia).

The city. Ur, royal city on the banks of the Euphrates not far from its outlet into the Persian Gulf, covered an area of six square miles. The huge size of this town does not seem to correspond with the number of its inhabitants, and we must therefore assume that when a family died out the family home was simply walled up and abandoned.

Far from being a model metropolis, smelly Ur had neither sewers nor paved streets—though at the same period cities on the Indus such as Harappa and Mohenjo-Daro featured sewers along every street as well as residential plumbing: bathrooms and even swimming pools.

Houses. Nevertheless, the well-to-do in Ur lived comfortably in houses much like those which would later go up in Greater Greece during the 5th Century B.C., and still later in Rome. Usually rectangular, Sumerian houses

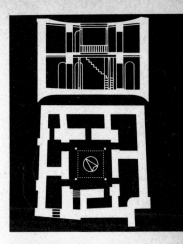

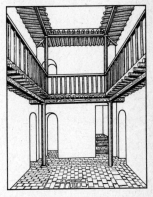

Ur: a Sumerian house, typical of building practice throughout the Middle East and Mediterranean basin. An inner court is encircled by small rooms. Only one door leads to the outside.

31

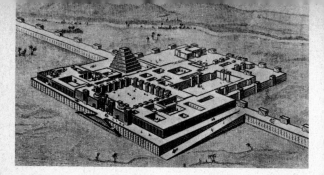

Khorsabad: a model of Sargon II's palace (722–705 B.C.). Covering 25 acres, it included immense rooms, courtyards and temples.

Susa: capital with double bull's head (Louvre), from the apadana, or throne room, of the palace of Artaxerxes II. It supported the cedar beams on which the terrace rested.

measured approximately 40 or 50 feet on each side. Only a single door in their tall white walls opened onto the street. A series of rooms on two floors had arched doorways opening onto a central courtyard. The roof sloped inward so that rain could drain into a pool in the middle of the courtyard—much like Roman residences of later date. Also sometimes there would be a small chapel or niche with an altar supporting a sacred statuette. A bricked family vault would be tucked under this chapel if it existed, otherwise under one of the rooms.

Assyria and Persia

Palaces. The Assyrians built awesomely huge palaces. Perhaps most colossal of all was one that Sennacherib put up in Khorsabad during the 8th century B.C. It had the classic ziggurat as well as winged bulls with human heads standing guard at the enormous entrance gate. The various elements of this palace, which covered an area over 1,000 feet long on each side, were built on a platform which towered 100 feet above the surrounding plain.

Another imposing kingly residence was that built by Artaxerxes II in Susa (4th century B.C.). Like the royal city of Persepolis (6th century B.C.), it typified Persian art as a whole, and tells much about structural systems of that period. Massive stone columns with a tremendous load capacity made it possible to enclose such gargantuan volumes as the apadana, or throne room, which covered as much ground as the Louvre's famed Cour Carrée. These columns, 50 to 65 feet tall and topped by capitals in the form of double bull-heads 19 feet high, profoundly influenced Roman and Byzantine architecture. King Darius could receive 10,000 guests in one room at his palace in Persepolis.

A pleasant feature which still lives on in contemporary architecture is the Assyrian use of flat landscaped roofs covered with gardens.

Persepolis: an overall view of the royal city started by Darius I (r. 521–486 B.C.). Palaces are grouped on a 32-acre terrace beside the mountain.

EGYPT

The fervent religious beliefs of the people of Upper and Lower Egypt determined the characteristics of a monumental architecture whose continuity over a period of two millennia remains unequaled in the entire history of art. Tombs and temples were constructed of stone, while sun-dried brick remained the common building material for humble human dwellings and even palaces.

funerary architecture

This covers a wide variety of different structures.

Mastabas. Last resting places for high officials of the Old Kingdom, these were neatly arranged in regular rows around royal pyramids, as at Saqqara.

Pyramids. Built as tombs for the Pharaohs and generally square-based, pyramids represent the very first stone architecture. The earliest pyramid, built by Imhotep at Saqqara (Old Kingdom), consists of six superimposed mastabas of decreasing size. Gizeh near Memphis can claim the hugest pyramids—those of Khufu (Cheops), dating to the 28th century B.C., Khafre (Chephren) and Menkure (Mykerinos), both of the 27th century B.C.

Hypogia were rock-cut tombs carved into the cliffs along

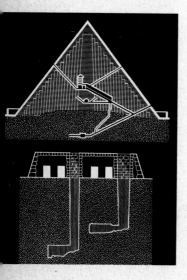

Mastabas consisted of two separate parts: a rectangular platform housing the chapel and a subterranean crypt, reached through a well, containing the sarcophagus. Pyramids derived from mastabas.

the Nile Valley. Galleries were usually horizontal and sometimes penetrated as deeply as 500 feet into the hillside. At the end a vertical shaft descended to the crypt. Best known hypogia are the tomb of Beni-Hassan and the Theban necropolis in the Valley of the Kings.

Funerary temples. Funerary rites for dead rulers were celebrated in these temples. The most remarkable temple was that built for Queen Hatshepsut at Deir-el-Bahari in 1520–1484 B.C.

divine temples

Largest of all was the Temple of Amon at Karnak. The ceiling of its vast hypostyle hall is supported by sixteen rows of 134 columns ranging in height from 42 to 75 feet, over an area 984 by 426 feet. Other ancient wonders include the temple at Abydos, begun by Seti I and completed by Rameses II in the 14th century B.C.; and the underground temples at Abu Simbel (or Ipsambul) which Rameses II ordered cut out of the rock. The main temple's entrance, flanked by four 75-foot statues of Rameses II, was raised to a new level to avoid flooding due to the construction of the Aswan High Dam. Also noteworthy are the Luxor

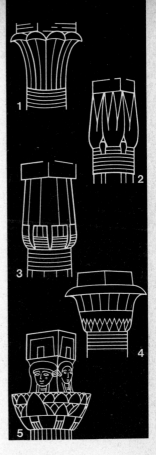

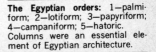

The Egyptian orders: 1—palmiform; 2—lotiform; 3—papyriform; 4—campaniform; 5—hatoric. Columns were an essential element of Egyptian architecture.

35

Gizeh: the Great Pyramid of Khufu, or Cheops (foreground). It is 479 feet high, with sides 754 feet long. Angles face the cardinal points of the compass. Precise calculations were required to establish the proportions of pyramids.

Abu Simbel. Cliff face is 108 feet high. Four statues of Rameses II guard the entrance. The temple was rebuilt on the cliff top during the work on the Aswan High Dam.

Luxor: the Temple of Amon-Mut-Khons (1408–1300 B.C.). The entrance pylon is distinguished by two statues of Rameses II and an obelisk. The plan is classical: a sanctuary deep in the interior preceded by a hypostyle hall and a colonnaded courtyard.

Deir-el-Bahari: the funerary temple of Queen Hatshepsut (XVIIIth dynasty). Partly built and partly carved out of the hillside, it is preceded by three stepped terraces with colonnades connected by ramps.

temple built by Amenhotep (Amenophis) III and the one Rameses III constructed at Medinet-Habu.

A marvelously preserved temple at Edfu (237 B.C.) went up during the Ptolomaic period, as did the island temple of Philae and the temple at Dendera. Famous for its sacred lake, the latter is the most intact in all Egypt.

A double symmetrical row of sphinxes and two obelisks usually fronted these temples. Their facades consisted of a pylon or trapezoidal tower fitted with grooves to hold flagpoles. Inside, the temples were designed to excite mystery and awe. One entered a court enclosed by a portico, and then a vast hypostyle hall which served as transition from the glare of the outside world to the dimness of the *naos*. As the latter was surrounded by other rooms, one's progress toward the sanctuary took place in ever-darkening gloom.

obelisks

These soaring single shafts of hieroglyphic-covered stone were set on either side of temple entrances and probably symbolised sun rays. Some obelisks have been transplanted to Europe and America. There is one in Rome at the Church of Saint John Lateran, another in Paris at the Place de la Concorde and a third, "Cleopatra's Needle," near the Metropolitan Museum in New York.

houses and towns

According to Diodorus Siculus, the ancient Egyptians considered their homes as being only temporary shelters on the long road to eternity. Consequently houses were not built to last, as were their temples and tombs where immortality lay.

The reconstructed plan of a house in Kahun, a city built by Sesostris II in the 18th century B.C., vividly shows us the general layout. It con-

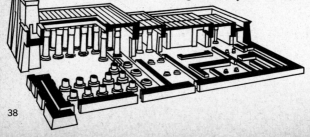

sisted of four parts: the living quarters themselves, with reception rooms and private apartments opening onto a colonnaded court reached through a long passageway; the wife's quarters with its own cistern; the commons, including the servants' quarters and kitchens with a separate court and pool; and the storerooms, workrooms and guest rooms.

A distinct change began to occur in the 17th century B.C. when sprawling "ranch-style" villas of brick and stucco arose in the countryside.

The houses of El Amarna, for instance, were much more spacious than older abodes. A broad vestibule led into a vast reception hall where the host received his guests and dined on a raised platform called a "divan." A lustration room where guests could freshen up faced the divan. The fireplace, a tile hearth sunk into the floor, spread warmth from the center of the hall. Here in the hall the ceiling was higher than in adjacent rooms to allow light to enter through clerestory windows. Private suites at the rear of the house radiated out from a room with a single column supporting its roof; this served as meeting place for members of the family. The bedroom adjoined the washroom which led to toilets fitted with fixed or movable seats.

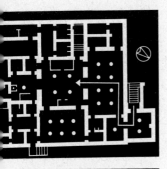

Plan of an Egyptian house. A long angled corridor leads to the courtyard.

Karnak: orthographic projections of the Temple of Khons (1198 B.C.). Built by Rameses III, it is a typical cult temple. A 52-foot pylon precedes an eight-column hypostyle hall and a sanctuary surrounded by small rooms.

sculpture

An inevitable characteristic of Egyptian architecture, as well as sculpture, was its monumentality. Striking effects were achieved through sheer size, though spiritual grandeur was also sought through simplicity. The statues of Rameses II at Abu Simbel provide an excellent example.

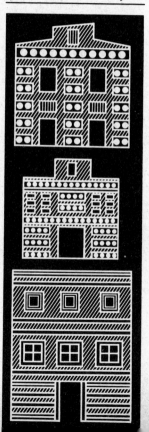

CRETE

Cretan culture, differing from others of its time in that it had no temples, was probably in large part due to Crete's being a fertile island ideally located midway between Europe, Asia and Africa.

Between the 28th and 15th centuries B.C.—that is to say, during its feudal period—Aegean art became increasingly important and its architecture can be distinguished by the shape of its columns.

houses

Houses, in which some Babylonian elements can be glimpsed, represent the first

evidence of this civilisation. Houses unearthed at Vasiliki (23rd century B.C.) were built of brick and wood on stone foundations and decorated with painted frescoes, while the less opulent Chamaïzi residence testifies to the feudal system under which Crete lived until 1450 B.C.

Palaces

The first palaces appeared about 2,000 B.C. Buildings dotted about a central courtyard followed the irregularities of the terrain with no thought of symmetry. Unlike Greek columns of later date, Cretan columns swelled at the top. Bathrooms and toilets were served by running water and an elaborate drainage system.

Knossos: palace of Minos. Notable for its internal complexity, it has downward tapering wooden columns and walls covered with frescoes on plaster.

King Minos lived in the most famous Cretan palace, sometimes called the Labyrinth, at Knossos. Its lively colored frescoes depict female attire and the island way of life some 1,500 years before Christ. A few small ceramic tiles dating from the 18th century B.C. show us how the houses of Knossos looked. Facades sparkled with many windows, an obvious advance over earlier houses which were completely enclosed. We know too that the interior of these houses glowed with brilliant painted frescoes.

41

GREECE

Greece's privileged position between Europe and the East made it a vital link between the two as early as the Achaean period (1600–1100 B.C.), though its real progress occurred in the last few centuries B.C. Though its major architectural remains do not antedate the 7th century B.C., we may still gain much insight on *pre-Hellenic* art thanks to the ruins of Knossos and the fortified citadels of Tiryns and Mycenae. Typical of Mycenaean art are the *tholoi*, or "beehive tombs", the first example of Greek encorbelled vaults. The largest of these is in Mycenae. Sometimes called the Treasury of Atreus and sometimes Agamemnon's Tomb, it is 49 feet wide at the base. The monumental bas-relief crowning the entrance of the Mycenae citadel (Lion Gate,

Mycenae: the vault of a tholos tomb, the so-called Treasury of Atreus (1325 B.C.), one of the first instances of a Greek "beehive" vault.

Mycenae: the Lion Gate (circa 1250 B.C.). The enormous lintel, with its column and two rampant lions, rests on a wall made of huge irregularly cut stones of a type known as "Cyclopean."

13th century B.C.) was carved from a single block of stone 10 feet wide and 12 feet high.

The Hellenic period, which includes all the monuments erected from the 7th century B.C. to the Roman conquest in 146 B.C., reached its apogee during the 5th century and the beginning of the 4th.

the Greek orders

Bases, columns and capitals comprised these orders, and they played an intrinsic role in Greek architecture.

The Doric order. In this, the oldest and simplest of classical orders, each element served a purpose and there was no useless ornamentation. Doric style flourished in the Peloponnesus as well as in the western colonies (southern Italy and Sicily.) As time passed fluctuations cropped up and the broad capitals of the temple of Paestum (6th century B.C.) gave way to the much narrower capitals of the Parthenon (5th century B.C.)

Some examples of Doric architecture:
—The Temple of Poseidon at Paestum (500 B.C.): six columns on the facade, or ''hexastyle'';
—The Great Temple of Agrigentum (480 B.C.): a pseudo-peripteral hexastyle;
—Temple of Zeus at Olympia (470 B.C.): hexastyle;
—Temple of Zeus on Aegina (470 B.C.): hexastyle;

The Greek orders: 1—Doric; 2—Ionic; 3—Corinthian.

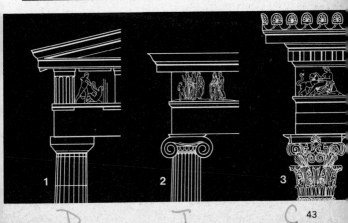

D   I   C   43

- —The Theseum in Athens (465 B.C.): hexastyle;
- —The Parthenon (447–432 B.C.), built on the Acropolis of Athens by Ictinos and the famous sculptor Phidias: eight columns on the facade (peripteral, octostyle);
- —The Temple of Apollo at Bassae (430 B.C.). The work of Ictinos, it combines all three orders—Doric on the outside, Ionic inside, with a single Corinthian column in the axis.

The Ionic Order. A product of the Aegean isles and the Ionian colonies on the mainland of Asia Minor, the Ionic Order found its purest expression in Attica. More flexible than the Doric, it evolved with time, though its

Paestum: the Temple of Poseidon. One of the best examples of Doric temples in southern Italy, it is beautifully preserved.

main characteristics were the two volutes whose curves could be accentuated.

Some examples of Ionic architecture:
- —The little temple to Nike Aptera near the Athenian Acropolis (438 B.C.);
- —The Erechtheum (420 B.C.) also on the Acropolis. It contains two peristyles on different levels and also the famous Porch of the Caryatids.
- —The Temple of Diana at Ephesus (330 B.C.)
- —The Temple of Apollo at Didyme (330 B.C.)

Athens: the Parthenon (447–432 B.C.). Built to house the cult statue of Athena, it was the work of the architect Ictinos and the sculptor Phidias.

Athens: the Temple of Nike Aptera (below, left), 5th century B.C. Though relatively small, its proportions approach perfection.

—The Temple of Athena at Priene (320 B.C.)

The Corinthian Order. This order was not very popular in Greece and was considered a variation on the Ionic. Its main characteristic was the use of small volutes above a row or two of spreading acanthus leaves.

Samples of this order are few in number and late in date but include the round temples of Epidaurus and Olympia (4th century B.C.); the small temple dedicated to Lysicrates in Athens (335 B.C.), and the Olympieum in Athens.

45

the Greek temple

The temple typified ancient Greek architecture. Essentially it consisted of a rectangular room (the *naos*) in which the cult statue was placed, and behind this room, another room which contained the treasury (*opisthodome*.) A colonnade or peristyle surrounded the building and over the facade stood triangular pediments. The only light relieving the temple's inner gloom came through the door—except for such temples as the Olympieum in Athens, which featured hypethral lighting, meaning that the main part of the temple lay open to the sky. Temples are usually classified on the basis of exterior columns:

1. *In antis:* temples have only two columns set between two pilasters in front (like the Athenian Treasury at Delphi).

2. *Prostyle:* a portico of four columns in front, as in the little temple at Selinunte.

3. *Amphiprostyle:* same portico front and back (Temple of Nike Aptera in Athens).

4. *Peripteral:* the temple has a colonnade around its perimeter, e.g., the Parthenon.

5. *Dipteral:* the temple is encircled by a double row of

Delphi: the Treasury of the Athenians (500–485 B.C.). Constructed entirely of white marble, this miniature Doric temple has but two columns on its facade.

columns, like the Temple of Diana in Ephesus.

6. *Pseudo-dipteral:* the width of the portico is doubled without there being a second row of columns: the Great Temple of Selinunte.

7. *Pseudo-peripteral:* has only attached columns along the length of the *naos,* e.g., the Great Temple of Agrigentum.

Although the temple with six columns across the facade (hexastyle) represented the most common form, there were many important exceptions, among them the Parthenon and the Great Temple of Selinunte with eight columns, the Great Temple of Agrigentum with seven and the Basilica of Paestum with nine columns.

1/300

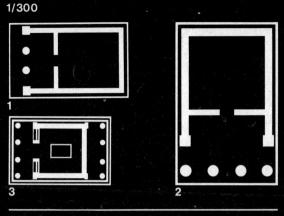

1

3

2

1/3000

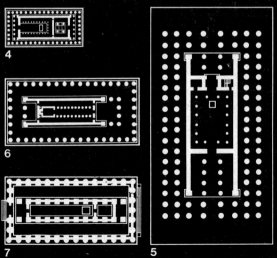

4

6

7

5

sacred enclosures

Temples were frequently placed within sacred enclosures, or *temenos,* which included a variety of other buildings. Thus the Acropolis of Athens, preceded by Mnesicles' Propylaea, the picture gallery and the Temple of Nike Aptera, contained the Parthenon, the Erechtheum and a colossal statue of Athena, as well as several smaller enclosures in which many statues and bas-reliefs have been found. Also highly venerated were the sacred enclosures at Delphi and Olympia.

civil architecture

Theatres. Though occasionally used for religious processions, theatres were more typical of Greek civil architecture as a whole. They differed radically from Roman theatres in that the orchestra area was very big and used solely by the principal actors and the chorus (Delphi, Epidaurus, Delos, Megalopolis). Other major examples of civil architecture are the palaces at Palatitza in Macedonia, the gymnasium at Epidaurus, the stadium at Delphi, the Tower of the Winds in Athens and the monument

48

Athens: the Acropolis. Literally the "high town," these fortified heights contained palaces and temples and looked down on the lower town which also was enclosed by walls.

Epidaurus: the theatre (350 B.C.). Designed to accommodate 14,000 spectators, it was cut into the hillside like all Greek theatres.

Ground plan of a Greek house.

erected to the memory of Thrasylus, the choreographer. Because of the Greeks' love of public meetings, many of their cities erected vast halls specifically designed for this purpose: the Ecclasesterion in Priene, the Bouleuterion (or Senate) in Miletus.

Houses: Housing conditions can be seen from a few buildings which have been excavated in Delos. These are rather small, but if we can believe reports of Greek writers of the time, there were also palaces with courtyards, galleries, libraries and rooms for guests. All houses in Delos consisted of small courtyards surrounded by a series of rooms with several attached wings, or *exedras*. The main room, or *andron*, was one step above the others, and received light from three bays of unequal width. The only entrance onto the street was through a single door. The *gyneceum*, where the women of the household lived separately, was generally on the first floor.

sculpture

An integral part of architecture, sculpture was essentially monumental in nature. Though carving on a Greek temple was strictly limited by the space available (pediments and metopes) there were nevertheless some wonderful exceptions such as the Porch of the Caryatids on the Erechtheum. During the brilliant age of Pericles in the 5th century B.C., the genius of Phidias, Polyclitus, Myron and Scopas all flowered. Phidias alone was responsible for the pediment of the Parthenon, the famous frieze of the Panathenaean procession, the chryselephantine (gold and ivory) statue of Athena in the temple itself, and the carving on the interior of the Parthenon and the Propylaea.

In the 4th century B.C., Praxiteles and Lysippus became forerunners of the Hellenistic period by creating the gigantic altar frieze at the temple of Pergamum. Color played a vivid role in architecture at that time and most temples were painted.

Athens: the Erechtheum, with the Porch of the Caryatids. In this asymmetrical Ionic temple, the columns of the south porch were replaced by supporting statues.

While Rome was said to have been founded in 753 B.C., architecture only began to flourish during the so-called Golden Age of Augustus, which started in 29 B.C.

Roman architecture's most typical feature was the use of rounded arches and vaults, though the exterior of buildings was decorated with columns in the Greek orders. In Greek architecture, columns were functional; in Roman architecture they were decorative. Professor van der Meer has aptly remarked that comparing the simple elegance of Greek temple ruins to the enormous remains of baths, forums and amphitheatres that the Romans built, there can be little doubt that whereas the Greeks were architects concerned with idealistic perfection, the Romans were merely (but superbly) great engineers.

Rome: plan of the Pantheon. A colonnaded porch leads to the rotunda, which is topped by a caissoned dome (141 feet high). Colossal scale and geometric simplicity distinguish this building.

Etruscan art

The Etruscan civilisation reached its peak during the 6th century B.C. in the area between the Arno and the Tiber rivers. Materially it had attained an eminent stage of development with neatly laid-out streets, well-planned plumbing and drainage systems, sculptured gateways (Perugia, Volterra) and temples set high on a podium. Vault building had become a high accomplishment and Rome was to be the ultimate beneficiary as a result of the Etruscan occupation (7th century B.C.).

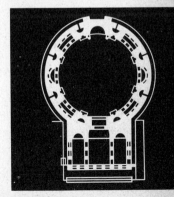

The theatre at Orange, France (1st century A.D.). The most splendid and best preserved theatre of the ancient world, it could hold 7,000.

The Roman Forum. Political and social heart of the city, the Forum was laid out on a symmetrical design. Its basilicas, sanctuaries, temples and commemorative monuments originally covered an area of 98 acres.

the golden age of Augustus

If we can credit Livy (Titus Livius), the Emperor Augustus built or restored 82 temples, and his successors, the Flavians and the Antonines (mainly in the persons of Domitian and Hadrian), kept up the good work. Rome changed drastically under Augustus but, after all, did he not boast that he had found it a city of brick and left it a city of marble? His reign could claim the construction of the Pantheon, the Baths of Agrippa (27–19 B.C.), the Theatre of Marcellus (13 B.C.), where the Doric order is topped by the Ionic, the Temple of Castor and Pollux (6 B.C.), and the buildings in the Forum of Augustus, with a temple to Mars the Avenger. Besides getting the aristocrats interested in Rome's beautification, wily Augustus persuaded them to encourage the arts and letters as well.

In France the first century of the Christian Era saw the construction of the famous

Maison Carrée in Nîmes, the triumphal arch and theatre (for 7,000 spectators) in Orange and that splendid, high-flying aqueduct near Nîmes known nowadays as the Pont du Gard.

the heirs of Augustus

After an intervening half century of upheavals, the Flavian emperors continued Augustus' work by building the Colosseum (75 A.D., technically the Flavian amphitheatre), the triumphal arch and baths of Titus and the Flavian palace on the Palatine Hill.

The second century A.D., from 96 to 192, marked the period of the Antonines: Nerva, Trajan, Hadrian, Antoninus Pius and Marcus Aurelius. They in turn endowed Rome with Trajan's aqueduct, the Ulpia basilica, the Forum of Trajan with the towering column commemorating his victories over the Dacians (113), the Temple of Venus, the Saint Angelo bridge, Hadrian's monumental tomb and the famous temple to Antoninus and Faustina. A few miles away, these emperors also built the port of Ostia and Hadrian's fabulous villa retreat at Tivoli.

Baalbek, Lebanon, the temple of Bacchus. A magnificent stairway leads to the monumental gate of the *cella* (shrine).

the Roman orders

Roman orders lack the importance they held in Greek architecture. Roman Doric, for instance, is much more refined. Its purest example can be found on the outer portico of Rome's Theatre of Marcellus which was started by Caesar and finished by Augustus. The Ionic, even rarer in Roman monumental architecture, is found mainly in the upper stories of porticos such as those in Pompeiian peristyles. The best known of these is on the Temple of Fortuna Virilis (1st century B.C.)

The favorite architectural order in Rome was the Corinthian, whose scale and rich decoration made it natural for columns rising 50 to 60 feet above ground.

Besides the capital itself, which consisted of a bouquet of acanthus leaves, the cor-

Rome: Temple of Fortuna Virilis (1st century B.C.). Raised on a podium, it has walls lined with Ionic pilasters. A portico fronts the facade.

The Roman orders: 1—Doric; 2—Ionic; 3—Corinthian; 4—Composite.

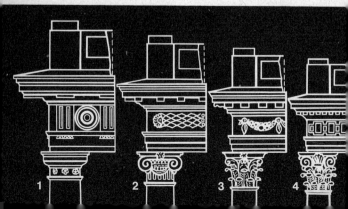

1   2   3   4

nice was also quite elaborate with friezes, coffered soffits, denticles, ova and consoles. Perfect illustrations of the latter can be found on the Temple of Castor and Pollux in Rome, while the finest capitals adorn the temples of Mars the Avenger, the Dioscuri, and Antoninus and Faustina, and the porch of the Pantheon.

At the decline of the Empire, Rome used a type of Corinthian capital which has been given the name *composite* in that it combines the Ionic with the Corinthian. The arches of Titus and Septimus Severus are splendid examples.

basilicas

These vast meeting places also served as courts of law. The general layout consisted of a high nave, two to four two-storied aisles and an hemispherical apse. Horizontal or gabled roofs usually crowned them except for the apse which was generally vaulted. Caesar built the most famous Roman basilica, the Basilica Julia, which had five naves each 360 feet long and 147 feet wide. Christianity copied this type of building in erecting its first churches under Constantine the Great.

Rome: the basilica of Maxentius (310–313 A.D.)—the nave (above) and ground plan. Thanks to the use of cement, the Romans were experts in the technique of the vault.

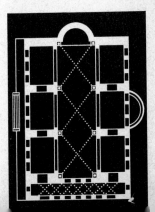

temples

Unlike the usually peripteral Greek temples, Roman temples were mainly pseudo-peripteral. There were, however, a few exceptions such as the temples of Castor and Pollux, Venus, and Mars the Avenger in Rome and the famous temple of Baalbek in Lebanon. The elimination of lateral porticos caused the development of the pronaos which became far more important than it had been in Greek temples. The fact that Roman temples were raised allowed grand staircases to be built up to them (to a height of 23 feet in the case of the Temple of Castor and Pollux).

Many temples were dedicated, not to a single god but to a trinity such as Jupiter, Juno and Minerva, and this resulted in temples with three opposing sanctuaries, such as the one on the Capitol. Furthermore, round forms were sometimes employed, as in the Pantheon, the temples of Vesta and Mater Matuta and the small temple of Baalbek. The Pantheon remains today one of the most striking monuments of its time. Its vast dome spans 145 feet and covers an area equal to that of St. Peter's in Rome.

the baths

Roman fondness for the gigantic can be seen in these structures. The Baths of Diocletian, designed to accommodate 3,000 bathers, sprawl over 40 acres, while those built by Caracalla cover 27 acres. These buildings included a tepidarium, or warm bath (Caracalla's measured 184 by 82 feet), a frigidarium, or cold bath, and a caldarium, or steam room. Annexed to the purely bathing facilities were invariably a gymnasium, palaestra (place for wrestling and other sports), a library and many store rooms.

amphitheatres and theatres

Indubitably the Colosseum ranks foremost as ancient Rome's most grandiose monument. Elliptical in shape, it has a circumference of 1725 feet and a major axis of 617 feet. The four stories of its outer walls are ornamented with superimposed rows of Doric, Ionian and Corinthian columns. Rome's oldest theatre is said to be the Theatre of Marcellus which dates from 11–10 B.C. Among other theatres and arenas are those at Capua, Verona, Pozzuoli, Arles, Pula, Pompeii and Nîmes.

Rome: the Colosseum. Also known as the Flavian amphitheatre, it was begun by Vespasian in 72 A.D. and completed by Domitian in 82 A.D. Its ellipse measures 617 by 508 feet and the four Roman orders are superimposed on its outer walls.

Roman theatres differed from their Greek counterparts, the latter being usually dug out of hillsides whereas the Roman variety were constructed entirely from ground level and the stands reached through sheltered galleries and *vomitoria.* A very beautiful and fabulously preserved ancient theatre remains at Orange in southern France. Built just before the Christian Era, it could accommodate 7,000 spectators, all shielded from the sun by an immense *velum* hung from the high masts dominating its facade.

Fascinating theatre ruins are those of the Odeon of Atticus Herodes in Rome (with a capacity of 12,000), and those at Aspendus in Asia Minor, Pompeii, and at Arles and Vaison in France.

commemorative monuments

Most famous commemorative monuments take the form of columns, triumphal arches and monumental city gates. The columns include those of Trajan (88 feet) and Marcus Aurelius (95 feet). Among the arches are those of Titus, Septimus Severus and Constantine in Rome, Tiberius in Orange, Augustus in Rimini, and Trajan in Benevento and in Timgad. City gates include Rome's Porto Maggiore and those of Autun and Saintes in France and Trier in Germany.

houses

The finest examples of Roman housing are to be found in Pompeii. Thanks to the lava which buried it, this city of formerly 25,000 inhabitants is remarkably intact. Like Greek houses, the Roman equivalent featured rooms arranged around an *atrium*, their only connection to the outside world being a single door not over 6 feet wide. Nevertheless they had a more inviting appearance. In some larger houses, a cloister (colonnade) encircled the atrium. The main drawing room where the master of the house entertained (*tablinum*) ranged along the centre-line while narrow passages led to the peristyle from which radiated bedrooms, or *cubiculae*, a dining room, or *triclinium*, the kitchen and storerooms.

We might also mention the Flavian palace on the Palatine Hill, Diocletian's palace in Split and Hadrian's villa at Tivoli, for such vast residences with frescoed walls and mosaic floors sprang up more and more not only in Rome

Rome: the Arch of Titus. Built in 81 A.D. to commemorate the capture of Jerusalem, it is decorated with composite columns and bas-reliefs. Triumphal arches were a Roman invention.

and Pompeii but all over Italy, sometimes appearing even in the provinces.

Roman gardens were landscaped architecturally with neat hedges and flower beds, tidily laid out in straight lines, raised terraces, cosy pavilions, pools and canals.

engineering works

Although essentially urban and decorative by nature, Roman architecture also had its utilitarian aspects. Some of its gigantic engineering triumphs still command our admiration, among them the Pont du Gard, the aqueduct at Segovia, the bridge at Alcántara, Spain, and two great roads in particular, the Via Appia (Appian Way), linking Rome to Capua, and the Via Flaminia, from Rome to the Adriatic.

sculpture

Less integrated with architecture than Greek sculpture, Roman sculpture nevertheless appeared everywhere on monuments, especially in the form of bas-reliefs on triumphal arches and mausoleums. It was also widely used in beautifying cities where equestrian statues stood at focal points of crossroads and squares, a custom to be revived in the royal squares of France.

Pompeii: a Roman house. Living quarters opened onto an atrium, or courtyard, surrounded by a covered portico.

Segovia: the aqueduct (98–117 A.D.). Such utilitarian architecture was gloriously Roman. Without mortar, huge granite blocks interlocked to form 128 arches 98 feet tall.

PRE-COLUMBIAN ART

Though several waves of immigrants poured from Asia onto the American continent between 25,000 and 20,000 years before Christ, the earliest evidence of a purely American civilisation dates back only to the 7th century B.C.

Pre-Columbian art concerns Central America and the northwestern part of South America. Cultures succeeded one another, notable for their ceramics and sculpture, and occasionally their architecture.

Chichén-Itzá: the Temple of Warriors, Mayan civilisation. Founded by the Itzá at the beginning of the 8th century, Chichén flourished during the 9th. This temple, famous for its snake-shaped entrance pillars, is preceded by the great esplanade of the "Thousand Columns."

Archaic civilisation of Mexico (1500 to 100 B.C.). This is mainly renowned for its splendid ceramic work.

Olmec civilisation, or La Venta culture, of southern Mexico (500 B.C. to 100 A.D.). It attained a much higher level of artistic expression: carved altars and steles and colossal stone heads.

"Civilisation of the West" (500 A.D. to 1521), along the Pacific Coast. This produced thousands of ceramic figures, some in polychrome.

Teotihuacán civilisation— "There where the Gods lived" (200 B.C. to 700 A.D.)—centre of Mexico. Here the first great architects built enormous temples, pyramids, palaces

The Pyramid of the Sun, Teotihuacán, Mexico. Built of adobe and 230 feet high, it is 787 feet across the base. A temple to the sun god crowns the top of its terraces.

and cities all decorated with elaborate frescoes (the Pyramid of the Sun and the citadel of Teotihuacán).

Zapotec civilisation (400 B.C. to 1521). This flourished mainly in the Monte Albán region, southern Mexico, and was remarkable for cut-stone tombs ornamented by highly evolved ceramic work.

Geometric decoration of the inner walls of temples and palaces shows tremendous skill and originality, and the interior of the Temple of Mitla, holy city of the Zapotecs, reveals an infinite variety of forms derived from textile designs.

Civilisation of the Gulf of Mexico (200 B.C. to 1521). Celebrated mainly for its sculpture, this civilisation also had an architectural style of its own typified by the Great Pyramid of Tajín.

Huaxtec civilisation (300 B.C. to 1521). This was another Mexican civilisation distinguished by its sculpture.

The temple and terraces of Monte Alban, Central Mexico. Built on artificial terraces toward the end of the 6th century, Monte Albán epitomizes Zapotec architecture.

The Temple of Mitla, Central Mexico. Holy city of the Zapotecs, Mitla is celebrated for its temple decorated with geometrically patterned friezes.

The Great Pyramid of Tajin, on the Gulf of Mexico. A very steep stairway connects its six levels; 365 niches have been cut into its exterior walls.

Mayan civilisation. In this case there were two distinct periods: from 317 to 987 in southern Mexico, Guatemala and Honduras; and from 948 to 1697 in the Yucatan, where it was finally submerged by the Toltecs. The Mayans produced the most impressive monumental architecture in all America.

Important vestiges of palaces and temples may still be seen at Chichén Itzá, Uxmal and Mayapán. Straight, steep steps led to temples perched atop huge truncated pyramids. The most refined is the

Temple of Warriors at Chichén Itzá. Palaces stood several stories tall and sometimes a round plan was used as at the El Caracol ("The Snail") tower at Chichén Itzá.

Almost all these structures were massively built and spans were short, as the Mayas had no knowledge of either the vault or the keyed arch. The only cantilevers in evidence were corbelled like the triangular "vault" in the governor's palace at Uxmal. Columns were sometimes used, as in the exceptional group known as the Thousand

63

Machupicchu, Peru: the citadel and artisan quarters. Typical of Inca architecture are the enormous stone blocks set without mortar.

Columns fronting the Temple of Warriors at Chichén Itzá.

Sculptured decoration abounded, the favored themes consisting of geometric designs, stylised faces or the plumed serpent.

Mixtec-Puebla civilisation (800 to 1521). These peoples in Central Mexico were master goldsmiths and ceramicists of the pre-Columbian world.

Toltec civilisation (800 to 1200). The Toltecs built such great cities as Tula, Xochicalco, and Chichén Itzá. Their art inclined toward the gigantic, as in the caryatids of Tula and the sculptures of Chichén Itzá. On the vast pyramidal bases of their temples, sculpture stands out.

Mexico-Aztec civilisation (1324–1521). By the time they were cut down by the Spaniards, the Aztecs had attained a very high degree of civilisation. This can be seen from the majesty of their temples and palaces, the richness of their precious jewelry and the expressiveness of their sculpture.

Inca civilisation (1200–1537). The Inca civilisation of South America flourished around Lake Titicaca and in Peru.

Artistically poor, Inca architecture nonetheless impresses because of its severe, military stamp. The walls of Sacsahuamán, the citadel of Machupicchu and the Temple of the Sun in Cuzco are famous for the mammoth size of the stones employed and the incredible way they fit together without mortar. Because of the imposing strength of their structures, the Incas were considered natural-born architects.

Indian architecture originated and still endures in the great ruined cities of the Indus civilisation (2,500 to 1,500 B.C.), the most important sites of which are Harappa, Mohenjo-Daro and Chanhu-Daro. Like the Sumerian cities, ancient Indian centers had progressed quite far technically. Subsequently, however, India suffered a series of invasions from the northwest, mainly by the Aryans, which retarded the development of an indigenous architecture. This evolved later, mostly due to the subcontinent's first unification in the 4th century B.C. and the advent of Buddhism in the 6th century B.C., since Indian art was essentially religious in inspiration. Buddhism in turn gave way to Islam, whose architectural forms adapted to local conditions during the 12th century.

Thus Indian architecture can be divided into three periods: Buddhist, Brahman and Islamic. Brahman art developed later than Buddhist, though Brahmanism, brought into the country by the Aryans, is much older.

Mohenjo-Daro. In this hub of the Indus civilisation (2500–1500 B.C.), archaeology has revealed highly sophisticated city planning.

Buddhist architecture

(250 B.C. to 750 A.D.)

Representative specimens of Buddhist architecture, in the form of stupas, temples and monasteries, abound in the southern part of India and in Ceylon.

Stupas. These domed structures, derived from tumulus tombs, were the sites of great Buddhist pilgrimages. Typical stupas are enclosed by balustrades and have monumental gateways called *torana*. Examples: Sanchi, Bharhut, and Sarnath.

In northwestern India, stupas on high square bases are crowned with several huge symbolic umbrellas. The Shah-Ji-Ki-Dheri stupa for instance in 394 feet tall.

Sanchi: Stupa No. 1 and detail of the door. Originally funerary tumuli, stupas usually form a dome symbolising the universe, with four doors representing the winds.

Temples, or **Chaityas,** derived from village sanctuaries. One of the oldest, the Gupta temple at Sanchi (5th century) consists of but a single cell preceded by a columned portico. Toward the end of the 5th century, the cell roofs were topped by a stone pyramid of flying buttresses with straight or curved sides.

The western Deccan is the site of many rustic temples, the oldest of which is the series of connected caves at Badami (578) and the most celebrated of which are the Ellora and Elephanta caves.

Monasteries, or **Viharas,** consist of a courtyard onto which open small cubicles and a sanctuary. Often they are cut into the rock, as at Ajanta or Ellora.

Brahman architecture

(from 600 onward)

The principal monuments of this type of architecture are temples erected on flat ground and no longer hewn out of the hillside.

Temples assumed their definitive form in the northern part of India and consisted of a sanctuary surmounted by a curvilinear tower or *shikara* with ribbed sides culminating in a sort of flattened cushion or gadroon, called an *amalaka*, which supported an inverted vase. The Temple of Lingaraja in Bhubaneswar is crowned by a shikara 180 feet high (11th century.)

Some Jain temples are capped with a superimposition of entirely carved oblong volumes, the most typical being the group of temples at Khajuraho (11th century). Over half the Jain temples have disappeared, but the most beautiful seem to remain. Among them are Kandariya Mahadeva, dedicated to Siva, and Lakshmana.

Bhubaneswar: the temple of Lingaraja (11th century). This plan achieves great architectural unity by placing a hall, antechamber and *cella* (shrine) in succession along the axis.

We must also mention the famous Jain sanctuaries of Mount Abu and particularly that at Dilwara (10th century). Made entirely of richly carved white marble, it can be considered one of the architectural wonders of the world.

The curious two-story Temple of Kailasa at Ellora dates back to the beginning of the Brahmanic tradition (760). This building, cut from a single huge block of stone, stands in the centre of a quarry whose depth varies from 50 to 180 feet. It provides an extraordinary example of architectural sculpture

67

or sculptural architecture, the two arts are so closely intertwined. In the south, temples are distinguished by the sheer immensity of carved gateways, or *gopuras*, which date back to 1100. Such temples are at Srirangam, Chidambaram and Madura, the oldest structure in the area being the temple of Brihadisvara in Tanjore (985–1018).

Ellora: Kailasa Temple (8th century). This monolithic sanctuary was cut into the side of the hill (above left.)

The Great Temple of Madura (8th century). The entire complex is walled and overshadowed by gigantic multi-storied gate towers known as *gopuras*.

Khajuraho: the Temple of Kandariya (circa 1000 A.D.). This gigantic stone mass is topped by a spire.

Sculpture. Relatively under-developed before the Christian Era, sculpture later became intimately linked with architecture. First expressed as narrative bas-reliefs, it soon took on more solid form, covering pillars, capitals and walls as in the high reliefs at Mahabalipuram and Ellora. Characterised at first by purity of form, balanced masses and harmonious proportions, sculpture quickly degenerated into excess and began to lose its finer qualities in the 13th century. Nevertheless the sculpture at Khajuraho, as well as that on the Black Pagoda at Konarak, is noteworthy.

Khmer architecture

This very special architecture finds superb expression in the glorious temple at Angkor Vat in Cambodia (12th century). Towering 165 feet over the jungle, with a circumference of almost 2½ miles, the ruins of this temple with its five main towers and moated wall were discovered in 1860 in thick jungle. Later its surroundings were converted into a park.

The enclosure of the royal capital of Angkor Thom contains one of the stateliest of Khmer buildings, the Temple of Bayon (10th century), whose porch has an undulating pediment representing the *naja,* or sacred serpent. This along with the lion was a favorite motif in Khmer art.

The temple at Angkor Vat, Cambodia (12th century). With towers, sanctuaries, galleries and porticos, the Khmer temples extended horizontally and skyward at the same time.

ISLAM

Moslem art was born in the 7th century with the expansion of Islam. A faithful reflection of this monotheistic creed, it opposed the polytheistic art of the ancient world and forbade the representation of living beings, the consequence of which was the absence of Moslem statuary.

The first work which can be attributed to this tradition is the mosque built for Mohammed in Medina in 622. Rudimentary as it was, it contained all the basic architectural elements found throughout the Arab world—a large walled courtyard and an interior colonnade, an oratory and rooms.

There are six basic components to a mosque:
1. The *mihrab*, a niche dug into one wall and indicating the *qibla*, or direction of Mecca.
2. The *minbar*, or elevated rostrum, usually placed beside the *mihrab*.
3. The *muhajar*, or balustrade.
4. The *pulpit*, generally of stone, on which a copy of the Koran rested.
5. The *midha*, or purification room.
6. The *minaret*, a tall tower with a platform from which the muezzin calls the faithful to prayer.

Other Moslem buildings include tombs, forts and palaces.

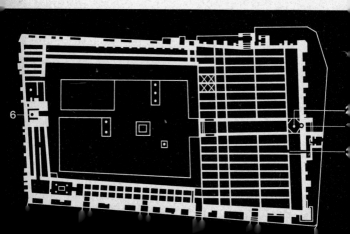

6

Islamic architecture—origins to 15th century

The Omayyads (of Damascus). Moslem art first reached its zenith in Jerusalem and Damascus, one of its proudest monuments being the Mosque of Omar, also dubbed the Dome of the Rock. Started in Jerusalem in 691 by Syrian workmen and decorated with Byzantine mosaics, it drew its inspiration from the round plan of contemporary churches. Nearby the El Aksa Mosque was erected during the same period, its elongated nave derived from a Byzantine basilica. The most august complex, however, is the Great Mosque of Damascus (707), built on a site formerly occupied by a temple to Jupiter and a Byzantine basilica.

Civil architecture of this period is represented by the Qocair Amra baths (711–715) and by such castles in the desert as Qasr-el-Heir (728) and M'Chatta.

The Abbasids (Baghdad). This dynasty, first ruling in Baghdad in the 8th century, is responsible for the Great Mosque of Samarra, with its helicoidal minaret, the Abou-Dolaf Mosque and the Tag I Kesra palace in Ctesiphon.

The Tulunids (Cairo). One of the very oldest of mosques (that of Amr or Amru: 643) was constructed in Cairo, after which the mosque character was drastically transformed by the advent of the Tulunids who introduced a Persian style. One of Egypt's finest Moslem structures, the Great Mosque of Ibn Tulun in Cairo (begun in 878), typifies this change with its cylindrical minaret encased in a spiral ramp.

The Aghlabids (Kairouan, Tunisia). The masterwork of this time remains the Great

Jerusalem: the Dome of the Rock (begun 691 A.D.). Built on the foundations of Solomon's temple, it owes its design to circular Byzantine churches.

Mosque of Kairouan (836). The arcaded courtyard is shut off from the outside world, and 17 deep naves are cut by one enormous transversal nave, making it possible for hordes of the faithful to face Mecca simultaneously in a broad front.

The Great Mosque of Tunis is built along similar lines, whereas the Great Mosque of Sousse resembles a fortified monastery.

The Seljuks (Persia). With this dynasty the planning of mosques was sweepingly altered. A domed oratory was built in front of the mihrab and four *iwans* (vast niches opening to the exterior) enriched the sides of the courtyard. The Great Mosque of

Cairo: the Great Mosque of Ibn Tulun (9th century). Cairo's oldest Arab monument, it has a horseshoe-shaped dome and pointed brick arches around its court.

Ispahan: the Royal Mosque (17th century). Its cruciform plan is extended by vaulted arcades covered with domes on squinches, a technique borrowed by Islam from the Persians.

Ispahan, rebuilt between 1072 and 1121 typified this new Persian type of mosque, whose influence spread to Syria and even so far as Spain.

The Fatimids (Egypt and Tunisia). From this period there remain the door of the Great Mosque of Mahdia (Tunisia), the El Azhar Mosque and the El Hakim Mosque

Córdoba: the mosque (started in 756). As shown here, Arabs often used ancient columns in building their mosques (below).

Damascus: the Great Mosque (begun in 707), Omayyad period. Built on a rectangular ground plan and with flat roofs, it is separated from the court by a colonnade of Corinthian columns.

(1003) in Cairo, the citadel of Cairo with its three monumental gates, and the palaces of the Qalaa Beni Hammad, particularly the Castle of the Lake. Decoration has Persian motifs and techniques: stalactites and faience mosaics.

Spain and North Africa. Persecuted in the East, the Omayyad emirs of the 8th century sought refuge in Spain. Abder-Rahman I, a descendant of the Damascus califs, took up residence in Córdoba in 756, a fact which explains the close ties in construction and decoration between southern Spain and the Middle East. His major work was the Mosque of Córdoba, enlarged several times between 756 and 987. Superimposed arches and ribbed domes, both of Persian origin, typify this building. The little Mosque of Bib Mardom in Toledo also has ribbed domes all of different design.

In North Africa the conquering Almoravides built the Kairouine Mosque in Fez and the Great Mosque in Tlemcen, while the later Almohades erected the far-famed Koutoubiya in Marrakesh (12th century) and the Mosque of Hassan in Rabat, the latter designed to be the largest mosque in the world but left unfinished.

Marrakesh: the minaret of the Koutoubiya (12th century), Almohad period. It is typical of Hispano-Moresque architecture.

Samarkand: Gour Imir tomb. These mausoleums superbly exemplify Persian architecture with their onion-shaped domes covered with glazed tile.

74

Among the fascinating aspects of Spanish and North African mosques were their marvelous square minarets. Those of the Koutoubiya and the Hassan tower in Rabat and the Giralda of Seville are justly honored. The Almohades also built the monumental gates of Rabat and Marrakesh.

Granada, Fez, Tlemcen and Tunis were the hubs around which the Hispano-Moresque art born in Córdoba eventually flourished. The oratory of Sidi Ahmed bel Hassan in Tlemcen, with its peerless mihrab, went up during the 14th century, as did the *medersas,* or theological schools, of Fez (El Attarin and Bou Ananiya) and the *zaouia,* or mystical centres, such as that of El Balawi in Kairouan.

Most prominent of all, however, remains the Alhambra palace in Granada (1334–1391) with its fabled Lion Court.

Egypt. Here, the first *madrasas* (the Egyptian equivalent of medersas) appeared in the 12th century. With a central court surrounded by students' rooms, madrasas were typical of the Ayyubid dynasty. Cairo can also thank the Mameluke sultans which succeeded them for many beautiful mosques, such as the funerary mosque of the Sultan Kalā 'ūn (1285), the mosque and madrasa of the Sultan Hasan (1356) and the Mosque of Kait Bey (1472).

Persia. When Mongols invaded the eastern part of the Moslem empire, they posed as protectors of the arts. Their finest buildings were the Gour Imir tombs in Samarkand and the Veramin and Gawhar Chad mosques.

75

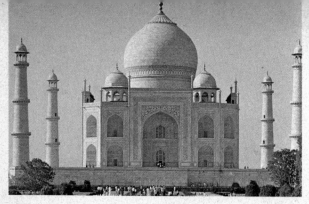

16th century

Palace of the Eight Paradises.

Persia, once rid of the Mongols, enriched its capital of Ispahan with esplanades, gardens and brilliant monuments such as the Royal Mosque (1612–1630). Many palaces arose, among them the Ali Kapu, Palace of the Forty Columns, and the

India under the Mongol conquest continued to put up edifices in the local tradition, as evidenced by the palace of Agra (1605). Most buildings, however, show markedly Persian traits—for example, the Mosque of Fatehpur, the Mosque of Lahore and above

Agra: the Taj Mahal (1632–1653). A shimmering onion dome tops this square building. From each corner of its base a slender minaret rises.

all the Taj Mahal in Agra (1632–1653). The graceful dome and minarets of this resplendent tomb built by Shah Jahan reflect their loveliness in a long pool.

Asia Minor benefitted from Byzantine experience in building Santa Sophia in Constantinople. Istanbul, as it was now called, soon became filled with extensive domed mosques preceded by a colonnaded courtyard and four tall cylindrical minarets in the Persian tradition. The Mosque of Sultan Bajazet (1501) and the Sulaimaniye (1550) in Istanbul are the work of the architect Sinan. A wholly Ottoman art succeeded this and subsequently flourished in Algeria (17th century), Tunisia (18th century) and Egypt (19th century).

Morocco remained impermeable to Turkish influence, resolutely constructing the

Istanbul: the Suleiman Mosque, or Sulaimaniye (16th century). Typical of the Ottoman school and obviously inspired by Santa Sophia, it is capped by a dome flanked by four half domes.

fine Ben Youssef medersa in Marrakesh in its own idiom.

Spain after the Christian reconquest was the site of a new tradition, that of Mudejar art. Its most unique monument is the Alcazar of Seville.

the Arab house

We know of Arab housing from several examples. The smallest house, dating from the 8th century, is at El Fostat, near Cairo, Egypt. The hub of this house is a courtyard, on one side of which are three bays of a portico opening onto three rooms, of which the central room has no facade. On the opposite wall of the court stands a niche resembling a Persian iwan. Pools, fed by underground pipes, adorn the paved court.

Usually there was a second floor reserved for the harem. While women were not allowed to be seen, they could look out onto the street from balconies enclosed with wooden scroll screens or *mouchrabiehs*, of which exquisite samples are found in Cairo.

Arab houses resemble Greek and Roman but with a difference—the entrance hall bends sharply to prevent indiscreet eyes from peering in.

CHINA

The Chinese can claim the world's oldest cultural tradition. It began during the second millennium B.C. in the alluvial plains of the Yellow River.

During the 3rd century B.C., the Ch'in dynasty united China politically, culturally and militarily, and built the 1,600-mile-long Great Wall to defend the northern part of the country. Between 100 and 200 A.D., China had direct contacts with the Roman Empire, and during the Middle Ages, before the Mongol invasions, it enjoyed a renewed period of greatness.

Chinese architecture's essential characteristic is that it reflects the continuity of this cultural tradition. Yet amazingly enough, few buildings antedating our own Middle Ages still stand.

The art of building depended mainly on the use of wood framing (pine or cedar), masonry being only employed in bases or subfoundations. The originality of the spatial relationships in Chinese architecture and its individual style devolve from its framing which, unlike the Western triangulated system, is based on a succession or superimposition of portal frames whose lintels allow the eaves to be projected far from the sides of the building. This makes possible a variety of combinations, so that the unity of Chinese architecture is in reality only apparent.

There are four types of roofs: pyramidal, hipped, gabled and an intermediary form between the latter two.

Another characteristic of Chinese architecture is its use of polychromatic decoration in which the predominant color is red.

Buildings are never isolated. They are integrated into complexes known as *compounds*, and their facades, overlooking a courtyard, generally face south. Cities (or large compounds) are laid out at right angles, with streets running north-south and east-west. The main gate is centered in the south wall.

religious architecture

Buddhism came to China from India in 65 B.C., bringing with it an architectural novelty: the *pagoda*. The octagonal brick Sung Yueh pagoda on Mount Sung Shan in Honan dates from 523 A.D.—the oldest monument still extant.

Also due to Indian influence are the Buddhist temples and underground sanctuaries such as the Cave of the Thousand Buddhas in Tun Huang (4th century), the Yunkang grottoes near Tatung in Shansi (5th century) and the Mai Tsi Chan caves near T'len Chouei in the Cornrick Mountains (6th to 11th centuries).

Among the oldest buildings still standing are the Tseu-En monastery with its Pagoda of the Wild Geese (652), the main wooden pavilion of the Fo Kuang Temple on Mount Wou T'ai in Shansi (857), and the Kuan Yin pavilion of the Tu Luo Temple at Tsi-Hien, Hopei (984). The last two are considered among the most beautiful examples of Chinese architecture. Also worth remembering are the Chen Mu pavilion at Tsin Tseu near Tai Yuan in Shansi (1023–1031), with its approach over a cruciform bridge; the pagoda of the K'ai Yuan Temple in Ting-Hien, Hopei (1001–1055), an octagonal brick building rising to a height of 262 feet; and the pagoda of the Fo Kuang Temple (1056), which is entirely of wood.

Thus the architecture of the period preceding the Mongol invasion is typified by the pavilion, with an interesting juxtaposition of masses combining vertical and horizontal buildings topped by a variety of differently shaped roofs.

Not far from Peking, the first city to be laid out according to a definite plan, and of which the largest part was built under the Ming dynasty between 1368 and 1644, is the circular Temple of Heaven with its triple roof of blue tiles. It forms an integral part of an ingenious composition of rectangular and circular enclosures con-

Peking, the Temple and Altar of Heaven (15th century). The circular temple rises on a three-tiered white marble terrace and connects with the Altar of Heaven by a 1,150-foot paved causeway.

Pagoda of the Kwang-Sheng Temple, Shansi. Brick-built and 174 feet tall, it took twelve years to build (1515–1527). Architecture and city planning flourished under the Ming dynasty.

K'ai Yuan Temple (1001–1055), Even its floors are brick. Octagonal and 262 feet high, it typifies the Sung period.

Loyang, the Great Pagoda (Wei period, 6th century). This octagonal brick tower is one of the oldest Chinese buildings standing.

nected by a raised causeway 1,150 feet long.

the Chinese house

Houses were generally large so as to accommodate the entire family, in the broadest sense. Thus it was not rare to see buildings designed to house more than a hundred people, domestics included.

The traditional dwelling consisted of a central courtyard, a large hall opening to the south and smaller buildings to the east and west. Bedrooms were on the first floor. The entrance was the only outlet to the street, the other buildings opening onto the courtyard. Some houses in Peking had two large courtyards, around one of which were

Chefoo: a private dwelling. The round door opens onto a courtyard around which secondary buildings are placed.

Peking, the Summer Palace— a covered gallery in the gardens. Polychrome decoration, with red predominating, typifies Chinese architecture.

placed children's quarters, guest rooms, kitchen and servants' dormitories. A spacious reception room separated one court from the other, on which opened the rooms used by the parents.

There were no chimneys. Heat was provided either by braziers or by a heated dais (k'ang) connected to the exterior by a flue and on which people could sit or recline and sleep.

The garden. In contrast to the architecture, which reflected rules of symmetry derived from the Confucian ideal, Chinese gardens express the Taoist doctrine. Here all is irregularity, asymmetry, undulation, curved lines, mystery and originality. Gardens are laid out to reproduce natural settings on a small scale by creating different levels, rockeries and water effects.

Man's presence is also hinted at in the form of pavilions, balustrades or bridges. Lawns are unknown, but cliffs, particularly of outlandish shape, are popular.

These were the ideals which resulted in the Garden of the West in Hang-Sheu, the Pei-Hai park in Peking (12th to 13th centuries) and above all the gardens of the Summer Palace near Peking, where most of the site is covered by a number of island-studded lakes.

Japanese civilisation is of relatively recent origin. The country had no unity until the beginning of the Christian Era and its art tradition harks back no further than the 14th century. Yet from that time until the end of the 19th century all architecture obeyed the dictates imposed by the natural calamities to which this region is subject: typhoons and earthquakes. Hence construction is mainly of wood.

religious architecture

Some ancient Shintoist sanctuaries date back to 478 A.D. Among the most important are Ise Naiku, dedicated to the cereal goddess, and Ise Geku, consecrated to the sun goddess. From these two buildings stem all subsequent Japanese architecture.

The introduction of Buddhism in the 6th century enabled Japanese architects to take inspiration from the Chinese, already steeped in a rich tradition. The Temple of Haiyuji at Nara testifies to this period. Other temples at Nara include the Shitenuoji, Ho Kyi, Hamji and Horyuji shrines. The latter, built in 607, is characteristic with its pagoda, gate and *kondo*, or pavilion, containing an image of the divinity.

Continental influence grew ever more important during the 7th century. Nara became the capital and soon was

---

Nara: the temple of Horyuji (607). A Buddhist convert, Shotoku Taishi built Japan's most venerable temple, which shows Chinese influence.

Kyoto: the Kinkakuji temple (Golden Pavilion), 14th century. The *shoguns* built this palace-retreat amid beautiful gardens.

dotted with palaces and temple-monasteries like the Imperial Temple of Todaiji. One of this period's most notable structures, the Sho-soin, or Imperial Treasury, built in 752, used triangular beams.

In 794 the capital moved to Heian-Kyo (Kyoto), where the Emperor and his nobles vied for the honor of erecting temples. Among those extant are the Yakushiji pagoda at Nara, the Daigoji and Sangen-In pagodas and the communal rooms of the Karyuji and Haryuji monasteries. This was the time of the Tsukuri style with its rectangular buildings sometimes connected by irregular colonnades winding through tortuous gardens.

In the 12th century a military government took charge at Kamakura, where Zen Buddhist monks strongly influenced local architecture. The vast temple rooms soared to lofty heights and materials employed became much lighter.

civil and military architecture

During this same era, the Samurai adopted the Buke style for their dwellings. These were encircled by a ditch and palisade, while various reception rooms, private apartments and domestic quarters were all joined under a single roof or series of roofs, the whole nestling under an enclosure. Wood and thatch were widely used.

From the 14th to the 16th century the *shoguns*, or warlords, erected such palaces as Kinkakuji and Ginkakuji set in carefully composed gardens, with delicately painted tea houses erected in surrounding parkland.

The venerable palace of Momoyama near Kyoto dates

The castle of Osaka (completed 1587). Of wooden construction set on a stone base, it represents the golden age of feudalism.

Kyoto: the Imperial Palace of Katsura (1620). Shown here are the library and music room of a sublime example of classic Japanese architecture.

---

from the 16th century, as do the feudal castles of Osaka, Edo, Himeji, Shibata and Matzumoto. Those of Nijo, at Kyoto, and of Nagoya came later (1603–1611.) Moats encircled all these castles which were built of wood and rested on stone walls.

During the 17th century the capital again moved to Edo (Tokyo), and here a great castle was built which now forms part of the present Imperial Palace. This age was also marked by the advent of the Imperial Palace at Katsura, perhaps the most representative building in all Japanese architecture.

Today Japan is booming and has produced one of the foremost architects of modern times: Kenzo Tangé, creator of the Peace Centre in the city of Hiroshima.

THE MIDDLE AGES

Just what were the Middle Ages? Historically, they spanned the interim between the Roman Empire's breakup in 395 A.D. and Mohammed II's capture of Constantinople in 1453. Artistically, the Middle Ages could be said to continue on to the Reformation (1517). Thus this epoch, running from the 5th to the 16th century, encompasses Merovingian, Carolingian, Romanesque and Gothic art. Christianity existed before the Middle Ages, however, and changed the entire face of the crumbling ancient world. It brought a new conception of the universe which was to bring about a revolutionary metamorphosis in art. A new architecture then appeared in Rome, and the new religion was celebrated in Constantinian basilicas whose rectangular floor plans resembled the great public buildings of pagan Rome. But the first synthesis of the ancient tradition and Christian thought took place in Byzantium under the reign (527–565) of Justinian.

Mont-Saint-Michel. This fortress-monastery, a symbol of medieval Christianity, rises above the tides. Started in 1023, the church was completed between 1070 and 1080, the choir being added in the 15th century. The monastic complex of the Merveille section, on the north, dates from the 13th century.

BYZANTIUM AND RUSSIA

Just after Christianity was officially adopted by the Roman Empire there occurred a break between East and West which was not only political and linguistic but ritualistic and artistic as well. While Roman culture all but vanished in the West, it prospered and even expanded in the East until 1453. The

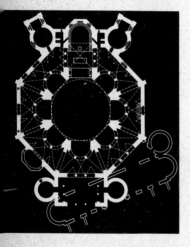

Ravenna: San Vitale (526–536). Its Byzantine-influenced plan features a double octagon with a long choir on the west and a dome on pendentives.

West had to seek new means of artistic expression, a search which eventually led to Gothic art, but it should never be forgotten that Europe was subject to Eastern influence for almost seven centuries.

Constantinople, or Byzantium if you will, had become the new Rome; Byzantines considered themselves the natural heirs of Hellenic civilisation, the now-Christian Roman Empire and the seat of orthodox religion.

Byzantine art manifested itself in the 4th and 5th centuries in the Greek-oriented cities of Egypt, Syria, Asia Minor and eastern Anatolia. Of Syrian architecture there remains only the ruins of the church of St Simeon Stylite, but the churches of Asia Minor had a certain influence on European architecture, notably on the basilica of Saint Demetrius in Salonika and the tomb of Galla Placidia in Ravenna. While the Western Latin countries continued to construct along the classic longitudinal plan, a great change had occurred in the East with

Ravenna: San Vitale. Windows under the dome illuminate the interior's rich mosaics.

Istanbul: Santa Sophia (532–538), the first of all domed basilicas. Spanning 101 feet and soaring to a height of 177 feet, its dome rises from pendentives and four enormous pillars above the square crossing.

the Byzantine creation of the domed basilica.

the age of Justinian

Naturally enough, the masterpiece of Byzantine architecture is to be found in Constantinople (Istanbul). The Church of the Holy Wisdom, or Santa Sophia, was the work of Anthemius of Tralles and Isidorus of Miletus. An amazing synthesis of the basilical plan and the dome, this square edifice, built over a period of only five years, stood unrivalled during the millennium of Byzantium's supremacy. The main dome, built on pendentives and 108 feet across, rises 180 feet above ground level over 40 matched windows. Its dazzlingly rich interior glitters with coloured marbles and mosaics, silver columns and a gilded and bejewelled altar. The same architects conceived the Church of the Holy Apostles, built on a Byzantine Greek cross plan. Unfortunately the Turks destroyed it, but its influence is seen in Saint Mark's in Venice and Saint Front's in Périgueux.

Italy furnishes several illustrations of how Byzantine art flourished in the West

89

during the 6th century. Supreme examples are in Ravenna: the basilicas of San Apollinare Nuovo and San Apollinare in Classe and the octagonal church of San Vitale. Ravenna also houses the 6th century's most exquisite mosaics, especially those showing Justinian, Theodora and their retinues.

Defeat and discord marked the end of the age of Justinian, when the Iconoclasts systematically and ruthlessly destroyed irreplaceable masterpieces of early religious art. Self-exiled artists then moved to Rome where they executed beautiful mosaics like those in Santa Maria Domenica.

the Byzantine renaissance

Happily a Byzantine renaissance began with the advent of Basil I in 867 and this lasted well into the 12th century. The Nea, or New, church of Constantinople characterised this period. Though no longer standing, the church's plan is known. It formed a Greek cross within a square topped by a central dome surrounded by four smaller domes all covered in Roman tile. On the eastern side was an apse flanked by two smaller apsidal chapels. The Church of the Holy Apostles in Salonika follows the same layout.

Salonika: church of the Holy Apostles (about 1312). A Greek cross inscribed in a square was used as a plan. Exterior is of polychrome tile.

Novgorod: Saint Sophia (1045–1062). The typically Russian bulb-shaped dome first appeared in Novgorod, a city not occupied by the Mongols.

Russia

Byzantine art expanded northward during the 11th and 12th centuries. Russia's wooden churches were replaced by stone ones, the first being Saint Sophia in Kiev (1018–1037), where the central dome is ringed by twelve smaller ones, thus symbolising Christ and his twelve apostles. Though of Byzantine design, the Russian flavour of the structure could already be seen in the affirmation of its vertical lines.

The Byzantine influence in Russia continued up to the Mongol invasion (1240) in such churches as the Desyatinnaya in Kiev, the Church of the Transfiguration in Chernigov (1017) and the renowned dome-topped churches of Novgorod: Saint Sophia (1062), Saint Nicholas (1113), the Church of the Nativity of the Virgin (1117) and the church of the monastery of Saint George (1119).

Italy

The 11th century also saw a Byzantine renaissance in Italy with the cathedral of Torcello and above all with Saint Mark's in Venice (1063–1073), "the Golden Church", built on a central plan and

Venice: Saint Mark's (1063–1073). The central dome is flanked by four smaller domes over each arm of a Greek cross.

whose narthex and domes are covered with splendid gilded mosaics.

Sicily in the 12th century was ruled by Norman princes who built a series of strikingly different churches throughout the island. Among the most famous of these churches—whose sole trait in common was the use of Byzantine mosaics as decoration—are the Palatine Chapel in Palermo and the cathedral of Monreale. Sicily's astonishing diversity of forms can be explained by the fact that Byzantine, Arab and Norman influences all met there.

THE CAROLINGIAN RENAISSANCE

After the aeon of upheavals known as the Dark Ages, three historic events led to the Carolingian renaissance: the conversion of the barbarians, the birth of the Romantic languages and Charles Martel's victory over the Arabs at Poitiers in 732. The movement's force was such that it soon outdistanced both Byzantium and the Arab world.

Though German by birth, Charlemagne grew up in the Latin tradition. He re-established the Roman Empire of the West, creating a climate favorable to the rebirth of western culture. His decree to rebuild all monuments which had been destroyed by war, invasion or fire was carried out, though oftener in wood than in stone. This was the German way of construction and it explains why so little remains today, the exceptions being a few big churches which required stone walls for structural reasons.

Thus we can say that while Charlemagne re-established Europe and gave fresh impetus to the Latin language, he also Germanised his empire by absorbing Germany and thereby paved the way for new barbarian onslaughts of the 10th century. Hence the Dark Ages which had preceded his reign returned after his death to spread over the entire West.

The main seats of the Carolingian renaissance were the abbeys of Tours, Hautvilliers, Centula (on the Somme), Ferrières, Auxerre, Saint Denis and Corbie, all in France; and the abbeys of Fulda, Saint Gall, Reichenau and Korvey in Germany.

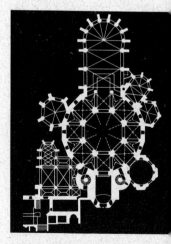

Plan of the Palatine Chapel (792–805), cathedral of Aix-la-Chapelle.

Germigny-des-Prés (9th–11th centuries). Built on a Greek cross plan, it shows Armenian influences.

Ottmarsheim church (11th century). This church's octagonal plan and tall arcades are derived from the Palatine Chapel of Aix-la-Chapelle.

From this brilliant period only one building of major importance survives: the Palatine Chapel of Aix-la-Chapelle (792–805), which was formerly connected to the imperial throne room by a 393-foot-long gallery. Its plan resembles that of San Vitale in Ravenna.

Other German examples of Carolingian architecture are the church of Saint Michael of Fulda (822), the entrance pavilion of the abbey of Lorsch (774), and the porch of the church at Korvey (885) in the Rhineland, while the most satisfying French specimen is the church of Germigny-des-Prés near Orléans.

Germany: portal of Lorsch Abbey (about 810) in the upper Rhine Valley. Its painted arcades recall wooden construction rather than stone.

93

ROMANESQUE ARCHITECTURE

After a period of unrest caused by successive invasions of Normans, Hungarians and Saracens, relative peace returned to Europe in the 9th century.

The artistic tradition born at that time was known as Romanesque (from the Latin *Romanus*) because of elements borrowed from Roman architecture, mainly the semicircular arch and the basilical plan for churches lifted from the early Christians. The sudden blossoming of this art form, which benefitted all Latin countries between the 5th and 12th centuries, shines forth as an integral part of the brilliant renaissance which followed the political and religious instability derived from the partition of Charlemagne's empire. The driving force behind this regeneration was Rome rather than northern or eastern countries, though distant lands did contribute as the result of pilgrimages and crusades. Religious architecture was the chief gainer from this movement, and "the world covered itself with a white mantle of churches."

The abbey church of Cluny (1088–1118). This 561-foot-long Benedictine church was the largest in Christendom. Destroyed for the most part, it contained two chevets, five naves and seven towers.

The pilgrimage roads toward Santiago de Compostela, starting from Chartres, Saint Denis, Vézelay, Le Puy and Arles, were dotted with churches modelled on Cluny, using the same basilical plan with apse, ambulatory and barrel vault. Some of the sculpture in these churches is remarkable. Pilgrim roads are shown in black, Cluniac establishments in blue, Cistercian in red.

ROMANESQUE ARCHITECTURE IN FRANCE

As Christianity expanded during the 11th century under the leadership of the great Clunist and Cistercian orders, Christian art automatically flourished. Spiritual power emanated as much from Cluny as it did from Rome, and in 1095, when the Pope consecrated the Benedictine abbey of Cluny, it was the largest church in Christendom. It exercised considerable influence throughout Europe until the 12th century, when the torch was passed to the Cistercians, who opposed the luxury of Clunist buildings.

Monks, architects and sculptors all turned to Latin countries for the inspiration of their monumental art, and the proof of this is found in Provence and along the Rhone Valley at Arles, Vienne and Lyon. Yet in other parts of France—in Auvergne, Périgord, Burgundy and Normandy—elements borrowed from the Romans or from more distant lands were adapted to suit the local climate and local tastes. The result was an astounding synthesis and buildings stamped with high spirituality.

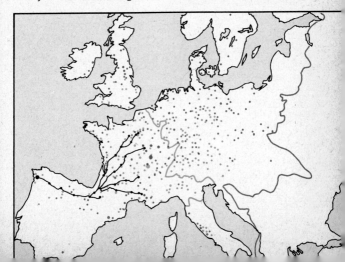

religious architecture in the 11th century

Starting in the 11th century, all Romanesque churches had several points in common: They were entirely roofed over in stone, either by means of barrel vaults, vaults on transversal arches, groined vaults or domes on squinches or pendentives.

These churches, which usually had more than one nave, could assume two forms: either a central vault higher than the aisles, as at Vézelay, or three vaults of equal height as at Notre-Dame-la-Grande in Poitiers. The vault of the nave and those of the aisles could also be different—for example, a barrel vault flanked by quarter vaults, as in the church of Saint Trophime at Arles. Barrel vaults could also be transversal instead of longitudinal, as at Saint Philibert in Tournus.

Their naves were considerably narrower than those of the old basilicas because of the difficulty encountered in covering them with barrel vaults. Walls also became thicker to resist the outward thrust of the vault.

The plan remained that of a basilica, but the nave and transepts were expanded, and apsidal or radiating chapels placed around the choir.

Treated as sculpture, the facade corresponded exactly with the plan, predominant lines being horizontal, in contrast to the verticality of Gothic architecture.

Sculpture was considered an integral part of the design and no church could be conceived without it. Sensitive and moving in the extreme, its several sources included Rome, Byzantium, Arab lands, Persia and even the Far East. The most magnificent examples of this work display themselves on the tympanums at Vézelay, Moissac, Conques and Autun. Some of the capitals and bas-reliefs also are genuine masterpieces.

Some very interesting early churches were built in Burgundy including Saint Philibert in Tournus (950) and particularly Cluny, now disappeared. Normandy also proved fertile and imaginative, erecting such edifices as the abbey of Jumièges, Saint Etienne (the Men's Abbey, 1066–1077) and Trinité (the Women's Abbey, 1062–1140) in Caen, Mont-Saint-Michel and the cathedrals of Coutances, Evreux and Bayeux (about 1077). The elevation of the nave generally consisted of three sections: an

Vézelay: Sainte Madeleine (1104). The groined vault of this Cistercian church is strengthened by polychrome arches.

arcade, a gallery or triforium and the clerestory. The first appearance of the ambulatory and radiating apsidal chapels, one of the essential elements of the Romanesque style, occurred in Saint Martin in Tours.

By the end of the century, a series of churches much like Saint Foy in Conques lined the pilgrimage roads leading from Ile-de-France, Burgundy and Provence to Santiago de Compostela.

the 12th century: the apogee of Romanesque churches

Romanesque churches reached their pinnacle in the 12th century.

Churches with barrel or groined vaults and without galleries. Three distinct groups of such churches are to be found in Burgundy:

The Cluny group, where the barrel-vaulted nave and the groin-vaulted aisles are not of the same height and the elevation has three stories: arcade, triforium and clerestory: Cluny, Paray-le-Monial (1109), cathedral of Autun.

The Vézelay group, on the same general plan but with a groin-vaulted nave and a two-story elevation: Sainte Madeleine in Vézelay (1104) and Saint Philibert in Dijon.

The Fontenay group in which the nave and aisles are more or less of the same height and the chevet often flat.

The churches of Poitou have precious little in common except perhaps for a tall tower over the transept and exterior as well as interior arcades: Notre-Dame-la-Grande in Poitiers. Some, like Saint Hilaire in Poitiers, were domed.

In Provence a simple plan was the keynote. Churches had no ambulatory and sometimes not even aisles; arcades were often parallel. Belfries consisted of square towers. Decoration followed the ancient Roman manner (Saint Trophime in Arles).

Churches with galleries (tribunes). These are found mainly in central and southern France along the roads leading to Santiago de Compostela: Notre-Dame du Port in Clermont-Ferrand, Orcival, Saint Nectaire, Issoire, Figeac and Saint Sernin in Toulouse. All these churches were characterised by ambulatories with radiating chapels and belfries on a dome over the crossing.

Domed churches. The oldest of these (1119) stands at Cahors and has two domes. Most of these domes were built on pendentives and buildings had no aisles: Saint Etienne in Périgueux, Angoulême, Le Puy, Souillac. Oriental and Arabic influences are especially noticeable, as in the Greek cross of Saint Front in Périgueux and the arabesque decoration of Le Puy.

Arles: Saint Trophime (12th century). The pediment over its porch shows how Romanesque art borrowed from antique models.

A comparison of the plans of St. Mark's in Venice (1) and the church of the Holy Apostles in Istanbul (2) with the Greek cross of Saint Front in Périgueux (3) shows the importance of the oriental influence to the domed churches of southwest France.

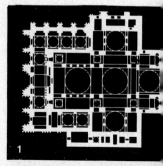

Poitiers: Notre-Dame-la-Grande (1130–1145). Turrets, structure and carved decoration typify the Poitou region.

Issoire: Saint Paul (11th century), typical of churches with galleries. Here the transepts are higher than the choir.

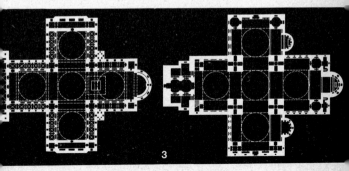

3

military construction

The oldest keep still extant is that of Langeais, built in 990. Outside France, the most noteworthy is the so-called Krak of the Knights (*karak* = castle in Arabic), built in Syria by the Knights of the Hospital in 1142. The riveting interest of these stone structures is that they perfectly express French military construction of the time and perhaps the entire feudal system. Most of these keeps are square. Round towers only appeared later, mainly during the Gothic period.

civil construction

Buildings could be of stone or wood depending on the region. In the first instance the influence of Cluny, Cîteaux and the Roman tradition manifests itself while in the second, limited mostly to the royal lands, the northern influence predominates.

Houses. In contrast to Roman custom, Romanesque houses opened onto the street, the court being reserved for domestic purposes. Often wooden balconies ran along the first floor, while the gable on the street and the stairway were shared by two adjoining houses. Merchant residences frequently had shops at street level and the ground floor was raised several steps above this. The entrance led to a spiral staircase rising to the first floor which contained the common room lit by small interconnected windows. Burgher houses differed somewhat with the main room on the ground floor.

Bridges. In this era of fervent pilgrimages, road and bridge

Syria: the Krak, or Knights' Castle. With most of its walls and twenty towers still standing, the Krak illustrates progress in military construction during the 12th and 13th centuries.

construction progressed remarkably: the bridges of Carcassonne and Albi and the famous bridge at Avignon, almost 3,000 feet long.

Educational buildings. All through history education had been the sole responsibility of the abbeys, but during the 12th century universities became independent. The University of Paris was founded in 1150. The Sorbonne, built a century later, had rooms for students.

Hospitals. European hospitals began during the 9th century. In France these buildings derived from monastic architecture and the oldest hospital, Paris' Hôtel-Dieu, dates to the 12th century.

City halls or municipal buildings. Until this period municipalities or civic groups used existing buildings put aside for their use by the local lord. France's oldest city hall is that at Saint-Antonin. If it is compared to the merchant's house in Cluny, with its arcaded shop in front, it suggests a large private home.

Saint-Antonin: the city hall. Oldest public building in France, it is nothing more than an oversized private home.

Plan of a merchant's house in Cluny, showing ground floor (1) and first floor (2). This Romanesque house opened directly onto the street.

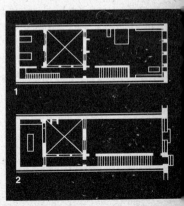

ROMANESQUE ART IN ITALY

Romanesque art developed in Italy in a special fashion. Each of the regional schools freely evolved according to its own traditions or whatever foreign influence might appear. Thus buildings of quite different kinds sprang up in Lombardy, Tuscany, southern Italy and Sicily.

Nonetheless the basilical plan was usually adhered to, and churches continued to have framed roofs. More generally built of brick rather than stone, their outer surfaces were often covered with marble.

Verona: San Zeno (1117–1138). A rose window decorates the facade of this brick building. The free-standing bell tower, or campanile, is typically Italian Romanesque.

The birth of Italian Romanesque architecture took place in Lombardy and Emilia.

northern Italy

This region's major characteristics were the cruciform columns, used for the first time, and groined or ribbed vaults, which first appeared in the church of Sannazzaro

near Novara. Frequently on three levels, interiors contained such typical features as polygonal domes over the crossing, exterior galleries consisting of small colonnaded arcades, tribunes over the aisles, as at San Giacomo in Como (1095–1097), and bell towers rising separately from the body of the church.

Milan's basilica of San Ambrogio, founded in the 4th century and rebuilt in the 11th and 12th centuries, offers a prized example of Lom-

Milan: San Ambrogio. A square atrium with a portico fronts the church (restored, 11th–12th centuries), and ribbed vaults were already in use over its three naves.

Pisa Cathedral (1063–1278). The campanile (1174), chevet and facade are all decorated with the same finely colonnaded galleries. At rear is the Leaning Tower.

bard art. A vault on ribs was used throughout the building, but even this precocious Gothic element fails to detract from the basically Romanesque plan of three naves prolonged by a choir with three apses.

San Zeno in Verona (1117–1138), with a wooden roof over the nave, provides the same arrangement with a campanile beside the facade.

Vaults built on ribs are also found in the cathedral of Parma (1058), as well as San Michele in Pavia (1100) and the cathedral of Modena (1099–1190). Exquisite arcade work embellishes the facade of all three. The cathedral of Lucca (1204) may also be associated with this group. In Como, San Fedele has a chevet decorated with a fine colonnade and a polygonal tower over the crossing.

Tuscany

The cathedral of Pisa (1063–1278) with its famous campanile (Leaning Tower) and separate baptistry forms one of the most admired architectural complexes in the world. The galleries of fine columns across the chevet and principal facade of the cathedral are repeated for emphasis on the round campanile.

During this same period, buildings were erected in Florence whose basic simplicity of form was masked by a complicated and geometrical system of polychrome mar-

bles. This city's octagonal baptistry, remodeled several times, well exemplifies this style. Subtly decorated San Miniato, built in the 11th century, dominates Florence from a hilltop and shows a wonderful blending of Romanesque and Tuscan art. Planned as a basilica with three naves, it too has a frame roof. Elegant green and white marble slabs, a typical Florentine refinement, cover its facade, which dates to the 12th century.

southern Italy and Sicily

In Apulia the Lombard influence can be felt in San Nicolas of Bari, an important church of pilgrimage, completed in 1132. The church has three naves and aisles covered with groin vaults.

In Sicily, where Normans replaced the Arabs in 1072, the structural elements of buildings, palaces and churches acquired a Norman aspect while the decorative features retained a strong Arabic cast. Typical of this mixture are the gabled arches and rosettas of Monreale. This melting pot, which also includes Byzantine traits, gives Sicilian architecture its striking originality. The ornamental sumptuousness of churches (cathedrals of Cefalu, 1131–1148, and Monreale, 1172–1189, as well as the Palatine Chapel of Palermo) contrast sharply with the rugged simplicity of Lombard buildings.

ROMANESQUE ART IN SPAIN

Like Burgundy, Spain led the vanguard of the Romanesque movement, and the Visigoths accomplished the transition from Roman to Romanesque between the 5th and 8th centuries (churches of Tarrasa in Catalonia). Starting in the 9th century, churches like Santa Maria de Naranco announced the birth of a new architecture whose development was unfortunately hindered by the Arab invasion.

Most of the churches in northern and western Spain show a great deal of French bias, mainly toward the Clunisian order, a fact that can easily be explained by the unceasing contacts that were maintained between France and Santiago de Compostela, site of one of the Western world's most famous pilgrimages. At the principal stages along the pilgrimage route to the Spanish city, new churches arose in which hemicycle apses, usually three in number, replaced the choirs with rectangular ends so char-

Zamora Cathedral (1151–1174). The high ribbed domes of Spanish Romanesque cathedrals show strong Islamic influences.

acteristic of earlier churches.

Spain's loveliest Romanesque church is certainly Santiago de Compostela itself (1078–1126). Its ground plan resembles some French churches, but its splendid portals—the Portal of Glory and the Portal of the Guildsmiths—are essentially Spanish, though a fleeting affinity to the sculpture of Languedoc can be detected.

Along this same road to Compostela stands the church of San Martin de Fromista (second half of the 11th century). Its three naves measure the same height, and again the influence in the architecture is predominantly French, though here more specifically Poitevin.

In the centre of Spain, the French-Spanish alliance against the Moors resulted in the construction of large buildings of a very special type, as exemplified by the cathedrals of Zamora (1174) and Salamanca (1160). Their ribbed domes set on groin vaults recall certain mosques and show Islamic influence. Naves are sometimes decorated in Arab style with horseshoe arches and chevets having superimposed blind arcades. This mixed Moslem-Christian style, known as Mudejar art, persisted in

Salamanca Cathedral (1160). Its ribbed stone dome is also typical of the Mudejar tradition which developed in central Spain. Among Spanish cities, Salamanca is one of the richest in monuments of all epochs.

Spanish architecture until the 16th century.

As far as sculpture goes, in addition to the portals of Santiago we should mention the cloister of the abbey of Santo Domingo de Silos (12th century.)

Military architecture took the lead during this period, the finest examples being perhaps the fortifications of Avila (1090).

ROMANESQUE ART IN GERMANY

In Germany Romanesque architecture was a prolongation of Carolingian and Ottonian architecture and it remained faithful to the old forms: double transepts and a western as well as an eastern apse. It developed mainly in those regions open to the advance of civilisation through the division of Charlemagne's empire—that is along the Danube (Ratisbon), and in the Rhineland, the home of several great cathedrals, including those of Speier, Worms and Mainz.

German Romanesque is quite distinct. Actually, just at the

Speier Cathedral (1156). Twin towers flank the apse. The cathedral's nave rises 125 feet.

Worms Cathedral (1016). Twin chevets and apses are flanked here by circular towers.

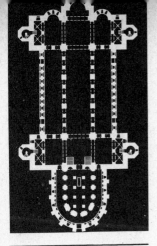

Hildesheim: Saint Michael (1001–1033). The Carolingian tradition lived on in its double transept and two choirs.

---

time that French principles were being defined, there appeared in Saxony those elements which were to sway Central European churches for two centuries or more. The first church built according to this formula was Saint Michael's at Hildesheim. Erected soon after the year 1000, probably from a plan of Bishop Bernward, it contains two transepts, two choirs, one surrounded by an ambulatory, and two apses. Supports of the nave alternate with two columns between every pillar, and there is a tower above each crossing.

The cathedral at Speier (1156) can claim one of the oldest groin-vaulted naves in Europe. Along with other churches in the Rhineland (cathedrals of Mainz and Worms and the Benedictine abbey of Maria Laach), it provides an excellent model of this style which is characterised by towers over the crossings of the double transepts, circular staircase turrets and double chevets.

Other typical features of Rhineland churches are their outer galleries, which run all the way round the buildings, as well as their use of "Lombard bands," a decorative motif brought to Germany by immigrant Italian masons. It is at Cologne that one senses the liveliest Lombard influence.

During the Middle Ages, Cologne, as the German Rhineland's great religious centre, inspired the building of many Romanesque churches. Pointed toward the Rhine, their apses frequently employed an unusual trilobed plan, such as the one in the church of Saint Maria in Kapitol (1030). Sculpture is almost completely absent from these churches and their stark block capitals are devoid of ornamentation or decoration.

ROMANESQUE ART
IN GREAT BRITAIN

The Normans, to whom we owe the magnificent abbeys in the French province bearing their name, invaded England to impose their way of life on the British Isles. Throughout the Middle Ages their building techniques dominated British architecture, and during the 30 years which followed the invasion of 1066 England acquired a profusion of cathedrals, abbeys and keeps. Of these structures, the most prominent were the cathedrals and abbeys of Canterbury (1070), Lincoln (1072), Saint Albans (1077), Ely (1090), and Durham (1093), the keep of Colchester and of course the beloved White Tower or Tower of London.

All the churches have three apses except for Winchester (1079), Gloucester (1089) and Norwich (1096), which adopted the plan of an apse and ambulatory.

The old square chevets to the east had disappeared temporarily after the Norman invasion, and their reappearance marked the return to Saxon traditions and the reawakening of a truly British architecture.

The decisive moment for Romanesque architecture in Britain occurred at Durham

Cathedral (end of the 11th and beginning of the 12th centuries) when a stone vault first was built over the nave. And, even more important, it was a vault on ogival ribs. This came late, it is true, as the building was started in 1093 and the vault only completed in 1130 after a test on the aisles in 1095, but it nevertheless makes this the oldest ogival vault in Europe.

Typical Romanesque ornamentation embellishes the arcades and pillars of the cathedrals of Durham and Hereford. Capitals are encrusted with foliage and animals, in a style which had been first introduced at Canterbury about 1120 and remained popular on the continent.

Only the sixty-three Cistercian abbeys, faithful to their creed, could be distinguished by their total lack of sculpture or ornamentation, but of these only ruins now remain (Rievaulx, 1132, and Fountains, 1135, both in Yorkshire).

Durham Cathedral (1093–1133). The first great building whose nave has ogival vaulting.

Durham Cathedral (nave): The disposition of the nave, like the geometrical decoration of the pillars, recalls the churches of Normandy.

Canterbury Cathedral (crypt). The first Norman church in England, it was enlarged during the 12th century.

GOTHIC ARCHITECTURE

The basis of Gothic, or ogival, architecture is a vault supported by crossed ogival (pointed rather than semicircular) arches, the vault's lateral thrust being absorbed by flying buttresses. This structural system, then called *opus francigenum* ("in the French manner"), found expression in civil, religious and military buildings throughout Europe for at least four hundred years.

Gothic architecture differs from Romanesque in other ways as well: its soaring verticality, its preference for open rather than closed spaces, and the naturalistic aspects of its decoration. Such architecture got to be known as Gothic through the use of the word *gotico* by the Italian painter Vasari. To Vasari the word meant "barbaric." He loosely employed it to describe all Italian art between antiquity and the Florentine Quattrocento (15th century), and he could not thus have referred to French architecture. In France the word Gothic became common parlance only during the 19th century, when readers influenced by such books as Victor Hugo's *Notre-Dame de Paris* naturally considered ogival architecture as so completely devoid of aesthetic value in the classical sense that they justifiably called it "barbaric."

Actually, ogival art is the tangible expression of a knowledgeable, dynamic and sustained civilisation. The archaeologist Camille Enlart wished Gothic art to be renamed "French art," regarding it as an art of pure structure without any false decoration; an art based on reason although executed by men of high spirituality. And it was certainly spirituality that launched those tall cathedral spires heavenward. In contrast to the cool calculated harmonies of the Greek temple, the Gothic cathedral symbolises elevation itself, in the religious sense of the term. As Le Corbusier so aptly put it: "The cathedrals were white, thought clear the spirit alive and the spectacle pure."

Notre-Dame de Paris (1163-1225). Typical of early Gothic, its horizontals are still strong, giving a squat appearance. Its west facade is dominated by two square towers, 226 feet high.

GOTHIC ARCHITECTURE IN FRANCE: 12th TO 15th CENTURY

religious architecture

Three separate periods can be distinguished in French Gothic architecture.

Beginnings of Gothic art: 12th century. Though crossed ogival arches did not originate in France it was in that country that the style developed, creating an ever-widening breach with the Roman-esque. Early trials were made in Normandy and took Durham as a model. The first large building using a Gothic vault throughout was the abbey of Lessay (Manche) in 1098; next in 1119 came the cathedral of Evreux. The first building in Paris to adopt this style was the abbey of Saint Martin des Champs (1135–1140).

A turning point in architecture occurred in 1140 with

Notre-Dame de Paris. Its interior, 426 feet long, 157 feet wide and 114 feet high, is divided horizontally into three almost equal stories. Sexpartite nave vaults rest on monocylindric pillars.

the construction of a series of large churches. They include the cathedral of Sens with its three arcades and triforium, a forerunner of 13th century cathedrals; the cathedral of Noyon; and, above all, Abbot Suger's Saint Denis, on the outskirts of Paris, where the true "Gothic" style was invented.

During the latter half of the 12th century the movement achieved real grandeur, radiating out from three major centres: the royal domain of Ile de France, the Plantagenet lands in the west and, lastly, Burgundy under the influence of the Cistercians.

Ile de France. The largest structures were erected in Laon and Paris. Rose windows first appeared in the Laon cathedral, and its nave rose to 79 feet. Later this building was imitated at Saint-Rémi in Reims, at Notre Dame in Chalons-sur-Marne, at Bamberg, Cologne and Mag-

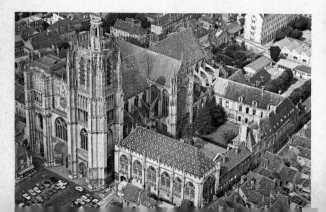

deburg. In Paris' Notre Dame, begun by Bishop Maurice de Sully in 1163, the height of the nave expanded to 105 feet, and it inspired the cathedrals of Mantes, Bourges, Le Mans and Toledo. Also in this group belong the cathedrals of Senlis and Soisson.

The Plantagenet domain. Here cathedrals did not follow the upward drive of those in the French king's territory. They remained rather squat, lacking as they did both

Le Mans Cathedral (1118), a flying buttress. These became commonplace in the 13th century to counteract the thrust of the master vault.

Sens Cathedral (begun in 1140), the first great Gothic cathedral. Its transept was added in the 16th century.

gallery and triforium (cathedrals of Angers and Poitiers).

Burgundy. Saint Bernard's rules called for simplified churches stripped of ornament and triforium; and Pontigny and Noirlac resulted. Though Saint Bernard's influence extended into Italy and Germany, there existed a major exception in Burgundy itself: the reconstructed choir of Vézelay, whose theme found Spanish imitators, principally in the cathedral of Avila.

Apogee of Gothic art: 13th century. Gothic art's most honored place names belong to Ile de France, Champagne and Picardy, the shining roster being Chartres (1194–1225); Bourges and Amiens, the latter the largest of all French cathedrals (1218–1235); Beauvais (1247–1280); Reims (begun 1211) and the Saint-Chapelle of Paris (1246–1248).

Choirs became increasingly important and complex: there were five radiating chapels at Chartres and Reims, seven in Amiens and Beauvais, eleven at Orléans and thirteen in Le Mans. The nave's elevation consisted of three stories and a triforium; pillars became more complex; capitals were reduced to a simple band; windows grew taller, broader and partitioned by fillings; the vaults were all rectangular.

The nave at Chartres soared to 121 feet, that at Amiens to 141 feet. Beauvais topped the record at 157 feet though it unfortunately collapsed in 1284.

The term *radiating Gothic* has been applied to the cathedral at Beauvais and to the Saint-Chapelle in Paris because of the way pillars have been transformed into a cluster of slender columns, each rib becoming part of an arch supporting the vault.

In fact, many 12th and 13th century cathedrals never got finished. Originally Laon was designed to have seven towers, Chartres eight and Reims six—towers or spires meant to intensify still further the exaltation of a sublime thrust toward heaven.

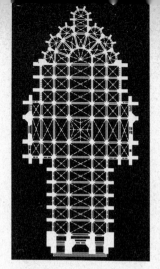

Amiens Cathedral (begun 1218), the apogee of Gothic construction. Its plan is characteristic, with a broad transept, ambulatory and radiating chapels. Windows are tall and wide, and the height of the nave (141 feet) was exceeded only at Beauvais (157 feet).

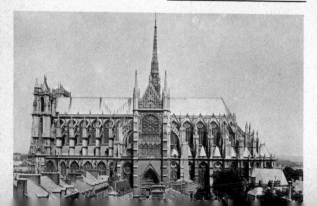

cathedral of Bayonne and Carcassonne's Saint Nazaire, were strongly influenced by those in the royal lands, though a single nave without aisles was also favored as in the cathedral of Toulouse. Interior rhythms accentuated by the use of buttresses can

Paris: the Sainte-Chapelle (1246–1248). A striking example of the predominance of windows over solid structure which epitomized high Gothic.

Reims Cathedral (started 1211). Its 270-foot towers accentuate the verticality of the architecture. Sculpture virtually covers its exterior.

Normandy, Burgundy and Alsace. Norman examples of radiating Gothic include the cathedral of Rouen, the Church of the Trinity at Fécamp, the cathedrals of Lisieux and Coutances and Rouen's Church of Saint-Ouen. In Burgundy the 13th century is represented by Notre-Dame in Dijon, the cathedral of Auxerre and the choir of the cathedral of Nevers. The cathedral of Strasbourg was never completed; we know that the original plans called for two tall slender spires.

The south. Churches of southern France, like the

117

be seen in the cathedrals of Saint-Bertrand-de-Comminges, Perpignan and Albi; and the church of Notre-Dame in Villefranche-de-Rouergue.

End of the Middle Ages: Flamboyant Gothic. The word flamboyant describes the flame-like curves and counter-curves of window fillings during this period when decoration tended to overshadow architecture, much as it would later in the heyday of Baroque. Copious examples of this very elaborate style can be seen in Saint Germain l'Auxerrois, Saint Etienne du Mont and Saint Séverin in Paris; Notre-Dame de l'Epine in Champagne; the cathedrals of Tours and Moulins, Notre-Dame de Caudebec in Normandy; Saint Maclou in Rouen; the choir of Mont-Saint-Michel and Notre-Dame d'Alençon. Brittany developed its own individual form with the cathedrals of Saint Pol de Léon, Tréguier and Quimper.

Gothic architecture lingered on into the 16th century with many transitional buildings such as Saint Eustache in Paris (begun 1532), the churches of Belloy (Oise) and Brou (Ain) and the cathedral of Auch.

sculpture

Sculpture retained the same importance it had held during the preceding period but with scale and idealisation both increased. Unimaginably rich in this respect were cathedral porches that were veritable sculptured Bibles; and awesomely beautiful details of Gothic sculpture are the Handsome God and the

Notre-Dame de l'Epine (started 1410). The curves and counter-curves on its flamboyant facade almost distract from its architectural beauty.

Gilded Virgin of Amiens, the Smiling Angel of Reims and Saint-Theodore at Chartres.

Stylisation totally surrendered to realism: human figures, animals and foliage were all faithfully reproduced. The Virgin took over Christ's place of honor over the cathedral portals in Paris, Chartres, Amiens, Reims and Strasbourg, all of which are dedicated to her. The same is true of the portal at Senlis, first of the great Gothic portals (1185–1190). Everything had become symbolic as well, each animal being given a specific meaning. Unicorns represented the Incarnation; lambs Charity; and pelicans the Redemption.

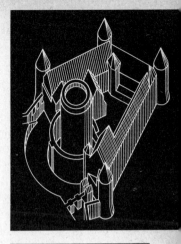

Coucy Castle (Aisne), drawing. The circular keep of this 13th century military masterpiece has walls 25 feet thick.

military architecture

The Middle Ages being a time of turmoil and frequent warfare, it is not surprising that city fortifications and castles advanced tremendously during the 13th century. Philip Augustus fortified many cities in the east and north including Paris, and crusaders returning from the east brought with them techniques which made possible the undertaking of impressive military works. Except for Carcassonne, Saint Malo and Aigues-Mortes, however, few Middle Age fortifications endure.

Ruins of the castles of Najac and Coucy, the latter considered a gem of its kind, also date from the 13th century.

In the 14th century castles evolved into fortified dwellings. Proof of this trend exists in the palace on Paris' Ile de la Cité; Charles V's Louvre; the castle of Vincennes; the Pope's palace in Avignon and the castle of Pierrefonds.

119

The advent of artillery in the 15th century had a still more potent effect on military architecture. As thick walls no longer offered any defence, buildings were opened out onto gardens, and windows and dormers increased in number and size (though towers such as those at Langeais, Ussé and Chaumont still persisted).

Finally, Louis XI metamorphosised his fortress of Plessis-lez-Tours into a comfortable country residence in 1463, and by that time Charles V's Louvre had also been converted to a vast and sumptuous palace. We might consider Mont-Saint-Michel as a military structure, as it began essentially as a fortified monastery.

houses

Houses of the Gothic period could be built of stone or wood or sometimes a mixture of the two. In the basically stone city of Cluny, Gothic and Romanesque dwellings stand side by side. Plans of both were the same, but openings in Gothic houses were much larger, their ceilings higher and facades better finished. Shops were on the ground floor, living space above and servants' quarters and storerooms in the attic.

Many Gothic residences of the 13th and 14th centuries are still standing in Cordes, a town in the department of Tarn; and numerous other examples may be found in such cities as Sarlat, Caussade, Reims, Avallon, Flavigny, Dijon and Provins. Rare in the south, wooden houses became popular in the north toward the end of the 13th century. Paris, Rouen, Beauvais, Amiens, Troyes, Caen and Lisieux contain even now frame houses jammed one against the other and jutting out over the street to gain as much space as possible. Large private homes had no less luxury than royal palaces if we can judge by Jacques Coeur's house in Bourges or the Sens and Cluny "hotels" in Paris. In general the roofs of Gothic houses inclined steeply in contrast to Romanesque. Upper floors were relatively open and their broad windows formed glassed-in enclosures, the only solid portion being the balustrades. Projecting bay windows also made their first appearance in the 15th century.

bridges

The work begun in Romanesque times continued with the construction of such spans as Orthez (13th century), Pont-Saint-Esprit (13th century), Cahors, Céret and Montauban (14th century). The Valentré bridge in Cahors was standard with its pointed arches, cutwater to protect the piers from floods and its three fortified towers to guard the passage.

public buildings

City halls. The best of these, in the north of France, featured a basically simple design —nothing more than a meeting hall, balcony and belfry.

Following the Roman example of Saint-Antonin, municipalities offered merchants shelter in the form either of simple sheds set against church walls, as at Bar-sur-Aube, or large wooden hangars such as those at Crémieu, Egreville and Saint-Pierre-sur-Dives, where the raftering is spectacular.

Hospitals were usually located near the cathedrals, though many private foundations concerned themselves with public health. The Hospice of Beaune, one of Burgundy's finest buildings, was one of these. Rooms for patients were carefully designed, especially as to ventilation: cases in point are the hospice

at Ourscamps and the hospital of Tonnerre.

Law courts also were built, one of the earliest at Grenoble. The court of Rouen remains one of the most dazzling buildings in that architecturally rich city.

Bourges: the Hôtel Jacques Coeur. A private dwelling built for Charles VII's treasurer between 1443 and 1453, it is nearly as luxurious as a royal palace.

121

GOTHIC ARCHITECTURE IN GERMANY, BELGIUM AND THE NETHERLANDS

Germany

For a very long time Romanesque architecture stubbornly persisted on the other bank of the Rhine, and German Gothic, which lagged at least sixty years behind its French counterpart, literally translated into German the style which had developed during mid-13th century. Thus Notre-Dame in Trier uncannily duplicates Saint-Yves in Braisne near Laon. Concessions to local taste can be seen, though, in the form of the towers and spires which are mainly fretwork, as in the cathedral at Ulm.

Lübeck Cathedral (begun 1173). It is framed by two splendid 393-foot towers.

Cologne Cathedral (1248–1880). This earliest German Gothic cathedral drew its inspiration from Amiens.

Ypres: the market hall. This famous monument with its belfry and carillon dates from the 12th to the 15th centuries. It has been rebuilt since suffering destruction in World War I.

The dispersion of the Cistercians greatly helped to spread Gothic art and the Burgundian influence asserts itself in the church of Ebrach in *Franconia, one of Germany's earliest Cistercian foundations. The Cistercians insisted on architecture of stark simplicity, the result being a flat chevet and the absence of a bell tower.

The noble German cathedrals made no attempt to dissimulate their borrowings from French Gothic religious architecture. The cathedral of Bamberg assiduously copied Laon right up to the decoration of its towers, while Poitiers inspired Minden with its three naves of equal height. Germans favored this system probably because of its plainness. Buttresses and flying buttresses were frowned on by German architects who, loyally adhering to solid structures, created the *Hallenkirche*, or churches resembling in many respects manorial halls.

The colossus of German cathedrals is Cologne, rebuilt, beginning in 1248, on the site of a 9th century church, after a fire. Its plan of ambulatory and radiating chapels derived from Amiens. Only by 1880 was it completed, still faithful throughout to the original 13th century plan. Number two in size is the cathedral at Ulm started in 1377.

Churches. Some, such as Saint Elizabeth in Marburg (1235), are a grab bag of motley elements borrowed from different parts of France. On the other hand, quite original are brick churches of the Hanseatic cities: Sainte Marie in Lübeck and Stralsund.

Sculpture. French influence pervaded as deeply in sculpture as in architecture, hence the striking resemblance between the statuary of Bamberg and Reims.

Belgium and the Netherlands

Brick was a common building material in Belgium and the Netherlands, and great hall-churches with tall, narrow windows appeared in both countries. The cathedral of Utrecht, Saint Gudule in Brussels and Saint Bavon (13th century) in Ghent resemble northern French churches, but the cathedral of Antwerp occupies a unique position thanks to its awesome spire.

Civil architecture thrived in exceptionally varied forms and cities tried to outdo each other with markets, guild halls and city halls abundantly and often floridly decorated inside and out. Municipal archi-

Belfry of the Bruges city hall (1377). Exceptionally ornamental in style, it well represents the "municipal Gothic" peculiar to Flanders.

tecture flourished in Flanders, home of the lofty bell tower. The oldest of these, at Tournai, dates back to 1187, and on its heels came Ghent's high spire.

Municipal palaces continued to go up well into subsequent centuries: Bruges, with its famous belfry, began in 1377, Brussels in 1402 and Louvain in 1447.

As early as the 9th century, Gothic arches appeared in Britain, the cathedral at Durham (1093–1133) being the first building in Europe covered with Gothic vaulting. English Gothic is commonly known as Early English, though of French origin, and developed by way of travelling Cistercian monks. William of Sens, a French architect, introduced Gothic to Canterbury and another French builder created Westminster Abbey. It should come as no surprise to students of architecture, therefore, that the double transept of Cluny is reproduced in such English cathedrals as Canterbury, Lincoln, Wells and Salisbury.

Nevertheless, the English modified the original ogival scheme by raising long thin naves and minimizing the importance of chevet. Avoiding vertiginous heights, English architects stressed the horizontality of their facades, especially at Wells. The lack of unity in British cathedrals can be explained by the fact that, with the exception of Salisbury, they were built in

Wells Cathedral (1220–1242). The amount of sculpture on its facade and on its twin, later Gothic towers is exceptional in England.

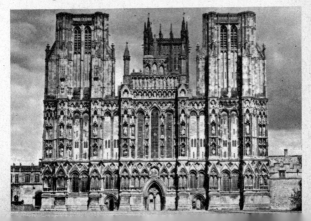

Lincoln Cathedral: the choir (1230–1280)—a foretaste of the *decorated* style which became popular in the 14th century. Arches are bigger, sculpture more abundant and windows more fancifully worked.

Salisbury Cathedral (1220–1258). A sterling example of *Early English* style, it has a double transept that shows Cluniac influence.

ever sprang out in all directions over the vault. Curves and counter-curves provided a foretaste of the flamboyant style. The *Perpendicular* style that followed was thoroughly and individually British. Horizontal and vertical lines proliferated and windows rose in an uninterrupted expanse from floor to ceiling. The cathedrals of Ely and Bristol show this trend. Bristol, for instance, begun in 1298, differs from previous churches in four major ways. It is a hall rather than a basilica and its vault ribs blend into the small columns on its piers. Vaults themselves assume star patterns thanks to the multiplica-

stages. Facades often bear no relation to plan, though in some cases towers rise forcefully, as at Lincoln Cathedral, and the use of glass is stressed at York.

At the start of the 14th century Early English evolved into a *Decorated* style wherein decoration took the lead. Ornamental ribs serving no functional purpose whatso-

tion of the liernes. Flying buttresses have been replaced by interior arches which, in crossing the aisles, create fresh opportunities for the appearance of compartmented vaults.

At Ely, novel spatial concepts were sought by crowning the octagonal crossing with a lantern, and tridimensional arches ornamented the lower walls in the Virgin chapel.

The pure Perpendicular made its debut at Gloucester (1330), where the end of the choir is one vast window. Its cloister also provides the prototype of the fan vault (1407). The Perpendicular developed with the Tudor monarchy and between 1480 and 1600 came to be known as Tudor archi-

Gloucester Cathedral (1330). The cloister shows an early example of fan vaulting characteristic of the *Perpendicular* style which carried on into the 17th century.

tecture. Its finest examples are the Henry VII Chapel in Westminster Abbey (1512), the Saint George Chapel at Windsor and, above all, King's College Chapel in Cambridge (1446–1515). But the curtain only fell on the Perpendicular with the construction of the hall of Christ Church in Oxford (1638).

Sculpture. Except perhaps for Wells and Exeter cathedrals, sculpture played a far punier role in Great Britain than it did in France. Similarly, in this period, monumental statuary hardly existed.

GOTHIC ARCHITECTURE IN SPAIN AND PORTUGAL

Though incisively marked by Islam due to the Arab occupation, Spain nonetheless remained receptive to Gothic influences from the other side of the Pyrenees. While Spanish Cistercian monasteries took after their counterparts in Burgundy, the country's churches drew their inspiration from northern French examples like Bourges, Chartres and Amiens. The cathedral of Toledo, begun in 1227, could claim kinship with the Bourges cathedral in its double ambulatory and double aisles. An architect from Champagne built Burgos Cathedral in the 13th century and also started the cathedral of Leon in 1225, using Notre-Dame in Reims as a model. Many Spanish churches still retain their magnificent cloisters (Pamplona).

In Portugal meanwhile, there arose magnificent buildings like the Cistercian abbey of Alcobaça and the monastery of Santa Maria de Batalha.

Civil architecture included such buildings as the episcopal palace of Tortosa, the fortified gates of Valencia and the city hall at Barcelona. It was during this same 13th century that the bright star of western Islamic architecture was built—the Alhambra in Granada.

Burgos Cathedral (1221–1457). Spanish cathedrals are direct offshoots of French Gothic cathedrals. An example is Burgos Cathedral, which is a near-reproduction of Amiens Cathedral.

GOTHIC ARCHITECTURE IN ITALY

Italy held out against the engulfing wave of Gothic architecture, and more than any other country in Catholic Europe it resisted the northern style. Instead of undergoing the customary Gothic phase, Italian architecture leaped straight from its own Byzantine-influenced version of the Romanesque into the Renaissance.

Completely at odds with the native taste, "gotico" remained confined to the northern part of the peninsula, and even there it offered a watered-down interpretation, as in the cathedral of Verona. Few naves were vaulted in Gothic style and even the arches pointed only slightly.

Of the rare Gothic structures in Italy, most important is the cathedral of Milan, which was completed only some two centuries after its cornerstone was laid in 1386. Its distinctively northern form can be attributed to the many immigrant workers from Germany and France. Its white marble facade, and indeed the whole cathedral, sparkles with pinnacles, statues and various other ornamental gewgaws.

Other Gothic elements can

Venice, the Doges' Palace. Typical of 15th century Venetian "Gothic," it has two stories of matched arcades which support a solid flat wall crowned by a light frieze.

Florence: Santa Croce. This Franciscan church was rebuilt in 1295. The nave rises 111 feet to the wooden roof framing, and a horizontal gallery runs all the way around above the arcades.

Milan Cathedral (started 1386), the most imposing Gothic building in Italy. The exterior is completely covered with an over-exuberant decoration of statues and pinnacles.

be found mainly in Tuscany. Most appeared in monastic churches such as the abbey of Fossanova (13th century), a faithful replica of a Burgundian abbey and the church of Saint Francis of Assisi (1228–1253). In this two-story place of worship the lower level's heavy and oppressive ribbed vaults contrast with the airy lightness of the single-nave vault above.

Another manifestation of this epoch's Italian Gothic took

its cue from early Christian basilicas, keeping their frame roofs and cylindrical pillars.

Central Italy gave birth to a quite different expression in the cathedrals of Siena (1200–1380), Orvieto and Florence (begun in 1296). Bricks were the basic building material, covered with polychrome marble.

Civil architecture ran riot, raising town houses, castles, palaces and above all municipal buildings. Gothic traits, though in evidence, seemed overshadowed by forms belonging to the early Renaissance. The Castel del Monte, erected for the Emperor Frederic II Hohenstaufen, reveals a curious mixture of French Gothic and Arabic ornamentation.

The Bargello and Palazzo Vecchio in Florence, as well as the city hall of Siena, stand as notable examples of municipal architecture. Perhaps Gothic's most original expression of the era is the Doges' Palace in Venice whose reconstruction began in the 14th century. Its delicately superimposed arcades well represent the florid Gothic which continued to flourish in Venice during the 15th century.

Castel del Monte. This octagonal castle was built in Apulia for Frederic II Hohenstaufen about 1240.

THE RENAISSANCE

What we call the Renaissance, a literal translation from the Italian *Rinascimento*, designates the literary, artistic and scientific awakening which spread over Europe in the 15th (Quattrocento) and the 16th (Cinquecento) centuries. The all-pervading Christian ideal of the Middle Ages gave way to a humanism marked by individuality and an enthusiasm for almost anything antique.

Many factors entered into the spread of the Renaissance, among them the invention of printing, which popularised ancient authors and engravings and made possible the publication of art works. Greek intellectuals fleeing Turkish tyranny brought many precious manuscripts to Europe, and far-flung travel became common as the continent's prosperity grew. And a new class of philanthropists and patrons significantly aided the arts.

This intellectual and political upheaval and the new demand for order and clarity naturally extended to the world of art as well. With the returning influence of Greek and Roman classicism, architecture came into its own again to dictate the development of the other arts. Consequently many artists of the time were triple-threat men—simultaneously architects, painters and sculptors.

The year 1414 marked a turning point with the discovery of a copy of Vitruvius' treatise in the monastery of Monte Cassino. Vitruvius, a 1st century B.C. Roman architect, called for symmetry and eurythmy, or measured proportions; and his manual with its precise descriptions of ancient Roman monuments became the basic text of all future classical architecture.

Naturally enough, the new movement originated in Italy where many Roman remains still existed. As early as the 13th century the sculptor-architect Nicola Pisano, in decorating pulpits of the baptistry in Pisa and the cathedral of Siena, drew his inspiration from antique sarcophagi.

THE ITALIAN RENAISSANCE

Three major factors animated the development of the Italian Renaissance: the return of the popes from Avignon to Rome (1449); the patronage of illustrious princely families and even the Papacy itself—mainly Julius II, Leo X, Clement VII and Paul III; and the taste for ancient literature and civilisation.

In architecture this revival manifested itself dually: in classic architectural orders and in domed churches.

The latter offered more of a challenge, for while the application of columns mostly involved decoration, the elevation of domes required designs whose proportion, stability and structural techniques called for careful and wide-ranging research. Later, French and then British architects proved to be masters in this field.

Florence: Santa Maria del Fiore (1296–1461). The entire building belongs to the 14th century, the only late addition being Brunelleschi's dome. With an internal diameter of 144 feet, its shape is reminiscent of a Gothic arch.

Florentine origins

As for architecture, the Renaissance began in Florence with Brunelleschi. The facade of one of his early works, the Foundling Hospital (1419), has a long portico of nine arcades resting on thin columns and decorated by round ceramic plaques. Also he designed in 1420 the beautiful dome of Santa Maria del Fiore, with its free span of 144 feet. Studying this dome, we might deduce that it was built by the last of Gothic and the first of Renaissance archi-

tects, for its slightly conical curve brings to mind 12th century Gothic arches.

In addition Brunelleschi built the churches of San Lorenzo (1421) and San Spirito, the latter started only two years before his death in 1444. The facade of Florence's Pitti Palace (started in 1441), for which he did the plans, is simple and elegant in appearance because of its massive stonework and arches.

Other early Renaissance names of honor are Michelezzo, responsible for the

Florence: the Pitti Palace (below, left). It was designed by Brunelleschi. The stone facade, measuring 721 feet long by 121 feet high, has great simplicity with its arches and embossed work.

Rimini: San Francesco (below, right), also known as the Malatesta temple (1450), a "Gothic" church revamped in the antique style by Alberti. The facade resembles a Roman triumphal arch.

Riccardi Palace in 1430, and Alberti. Alberti, who wrote an authoritative treatise on architecture, gave the Rucellai Palace the same spirit as the Riccardi, featuring rustication, twin-column windows and a jutting cornice. Florence's Strozzi Palace, started by Benedetto da Majano and continued (1489) by Cronaca, similarly features rustication as its architectural ornamentation.

Rimini's church of San Francesco and Mantua's church of San Sebastian are both Alberti creations. Florentine architecture spread through-out the province, and its influence overran into northern Italy in such landmarks as Fra Gioconda's Loggia of the Lords in Verona, Amadeo's lavishly decorated charterhouse in Pavia, the young Bramante's Santa Maria della Grazie in Milan and Pietro Lombardo's Vendramin Calergi Palace in Venice (1481–1509).

Venice: Vendramin-Calergi Palace (completed 1509). The main floor consists of bays between columns. Some decorative details are still Gothic, and the Venetians long remained fond of this style.

high renaissance in Rome

A golden name—Bramante—dominates this period. Yet Pope Julius II deserves much credit too, for he had the happy idea of bringing together the era's three brightest stars—the sculptor Michelangelo, the painter Raphael and the architect Bramante. Although Saint Peter's in Rome ranks as the definitive work of its time, it should not overshadow such other buildings as the Cancellaria, the cloister of Santa Maria della Pace and the Giraud Palace. The Tempietto (1502), a small circular chapel put

Verona: the Council House (1476–1493). Though Florentine art thrived in northern Italy, this building is closer to the Venetian style.

up by Bramante in the courtyard of the convent of San Pietro in Montorio, gracefully re-interprets ancient round temples, and the columns round its base are pure Doric in design.

Antonio Sangallo, the Younger, owes his fame to the construction of Rome's Farnese Palace (1530). He also built the rigorously symmetrical Pandolfini Palace (1516) in Florence. Still another architect, Peruzzi, has many

137

palaces to his credit: the Farnesina (1509), the Lante, and his masterpiece, the Massimi alle Colonne (1532) in Rome, and the Albergati in Bologna. About the same time in Venice Sanmicheli built the Grimani Palace, and Sansovino both the loggia of the campanile and the masterful Libreria Vecchia on Saint Mark's Square.

Roman mannerism

In Italy the Renaissance died hard and long. Whereas in France new forms had been sought on the heels of Henri II's death, Italian architecture continued well into the 17th century with works gradually transforming to a different style of expression called *Baroque*. Rome was the centre of its original development, and its influence spread throughout Europe and to England under the guidance of Palladio. While this style of architecture may seem inferior to that which preceded it, many great names guided its development: Michelangelo, Vignola and, in the 17th century, Bernini.

Michelangelo carried on Bramante's work at Saint Peter's. Primarily a sculptor,

---

Rome: the little temple of San Pietro in Montorio (about 1500). With its Doric columns and its cupola, this chapel by Bramante is an original interpretation of an antique circular temple.

138

Michelangelo turned to architecture during his late years and at seventy received the commission to complete Saint Peter's dome and the Farnese Palace. As architect, Michelangelo also sired the plan of the trapezoidal piazza on the Capitol centered around the famous equestrian statue of Marcus Aurelius.

Vignola began building Rome's Gesu church in 1584. This edifice, destined to influence Christian architecture everywhere for many years, inaugurated the so-called "Jesuit" style. Vignola also authored a *Treatise on the Five Orders,* considered by some as an improvement on Vitruvius.

Fontana, builder of the Sistine Chapel and Rome's most inventive city planner, laid out streets at right angles ending in squares decorated with obelisks and monumental fountains. Maderna (the eastern facade of Saint Peter's, 1606–1612), Galilei (the porch of Saint John Lateran) and Fuga (facade of Santa Maria Maggiore) all well represent the late Renaissance.

In Genoa, Alessi built a series of palaces as well as the church of Santa Maria at Carignano.

The towering figure of Palladio, creator of Vicenza's famous basilica, alone gave a spurt of life to the languishing Renaissance by building splendid villas in Vicenza and its environs. Perhaps the most magnificent of these is the famed Villa Capra, or Rotunda, a centrally planned structure with four facades decorated with Ionic columns. His most original work, however, remains Vicenza's Olim-

Venice: Grimani Palace (about 1550), built by San Micheli in the tradition of other Venetian palaces with ornate galleries. Its facade recalls that of the Vendramin Palace.

Rome: the Farnese Palace (1546) is typical of residences built in Rome during the high Renaissance. Michelangelo designed the upper floor and cornice **(right)**.

Vicenza: Villa Capra or "Rotunda" (started 1567). This centrally planned building has four colonnaded facades and, like Palladio's other villas, was based on ancient Roman residences.

Vicenza: the Olimpico theatre (started 1580). Palladio's most original work, it has a permanent stage setting, seen here in perspective.

Opposite page: above
Todi: Santa Maria della Consolazione (started 1508, completed 1607). A centrally planned church.

below:
Vicenza: the basilica (completed 1614). Palladio put this classical decoration over a much older building.

pico theatre, whose stage is a trompe l'oeil gem of breath-taking facades and receding city streets (begun 1580). In Venice his work includes such churches as the Redentore and San Giorgio Maggiore.

Saint Peter's in Rome

Saint Peter's endures as the crown jewel of the Italian Renaissance, an architectural marvel only equalled at Versailles.

The original basilica of Saint Peter's, built in the 4th century, was a frame-roofed structure with five naves rising over the site of Nero's Circus. Because of its tottering condition, reconstruction began as far back as the 15th century but work was subsequently abandoned. When Julius II decided to start over on an entirely new basis, he entrusted the design to Bramante, and the cornerstone of the first pillar under the dome was laid on April 18, 1506.

The original plan called for a central church built over a Greek cross with four identical facades, the centre crowned with a dome built on pendentives and supported by four smaller domes.

Upon Bramante's death in 1514, Raphael continued the work but elongated one arm of the Greek cross to fit a basilical plan. Raphael followed Bramante into his grave only six years later and a host of new projects appeared, including Peruzzi's Greek cross and Sangallo's extended Greek cross.

Then, at age seventy, came Michelangelo, who devoted

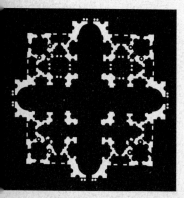

Rome: Bramante's project for Saint Peter's (1506)—a Greek cross with a central dome flanked by four apses with domes on the same plan.

Rome: Saint Peter's (1506–1626), the most important building of its period. The dome is the work of Michelangelo, the court and colonnade of Bernini.

142

the remaining eighteen years of his life to Saint Peter's. He took over Bramante's original plan, reinforcing the pillars under the great dome, flanking the exteriors of the apses with gigantic Corinthian pilasters and building a drum which allowed the dome to rise quite separately from the nave. Though he never saw the dome finished, he left behind complete plans for its execution.

His first successor, Vignola, worked only on the subsidiary dome and his pupil Giacomo della Porta finished the outside of the dome. Pope Paul V then decided to extend the nave to form a Latin cross, adding three bays and two side chapels next to the entrance. The facade, built by Maderna on plans laid down by Michelangelo, has the unfortunate effect of blocking any view of the dome as the building is approached. Thus Saint Peter's, which now

covers an area of some 161,000 square feet and measures 692 feet in length, was essentially a composite structure. It was consecrated only in November 1626, just over 120 years after the first stone was laid. The entire complex remained incomplete until the 17th century when Bernini, who assumed architectural direction in 1629, finished his oval piazza surrounded by a quadruple colonnade (1655–1657).

sculpture

This epoch's monumental Italian architecture would be inconceivable without its accompanying sculpture. The Renaissance began with sculpture (Pisano), and the sculptor's first concern was to plaster his works onto buildings. For example, Ghiberti's doors for the baptistry in Florence show exquisite workmanship. Thus a whole line of artists contributed their talents: Donatello and Verrocchio, Lucca della Robbia, whose enamelled ceramic plaques decorate the hospital of Pistoia, and Sansovino who did the sculpture for his own architectural projects in Venice. Nor should Benvenuto Cellini or John of Bologna be forgotten. Michelangelo overshadowed them all, however; even in his lifetime he was referred to as sculpture incarnate.

the Italian garden

Since the end of the Roman empire the art of gardening had slumbered, but with the construction of palaces and villas during the Cinquecento, new green spaces were planted which were to be emulated for the next three centuries. Among the most celebrated dating from this period are the gardens of the Villa Medici in Rome, the Villa d'Este in Tivoli, the Casino of Caprarola, the Villa Lante in Bagnaia, the Boboli gardens surrounding the Pitti Palace in Florence and the gardens of the Aldobrandini and Lancelotti villas in Frascati.

Italian Renaissance gardens were designed as extensions of the villas and palaces which they surrounded. Consequently, they were carefully laid out by architects along classical, well-proportioned lines and incorporated such pseudo-antique elements as grottos, pools, colonnades and statuary.

Enclosed by pines and cypresses, these gardens were arranged on different levels to accentuate their meticulously laid out designs.

THE RENAISSANCE IN FRANCE

The Renaissance did not sweep France overnight as the result of the Italian wars. For many years contacts had been established between artists of the two countries, and Italian craftsmen plied their trade in Paris, at King René's court in Aix and in Toulouse. Also French painters like Jean Fouquet frequently travelled as far as Rome. Furthermore the architectural revolution, begun at Plessis-les-Tours in 1463, continued.

Actually, Gothic art could go no further, and the flamboyant style which sacrificed structure to decoration had become a transitional form corresponding to the metamorphosis in both art and customs. Art tended to lose its mass appeal to become a royal prerogative, depending mainly for its support on rich patrons. In spite of an avidity for Italian "images", French medieval traditions held sway well into the 18th century. Traditional plans were followed, adaptation to the local climate remained the essential rule and building techniques inherited from the Middle Ages were still in common use.

Four major periods characterise the French Renaissance, each more or less corresponding to a reign:

Charles VIII (1483–1498): the application of antique decorative elements to Gothic structures (castle of Amboise).

Louis XII (1498–1515): the appearance of the classical architectural orders (Blois).

François I (1515–1547): the high point of the French Renaissance (Fontainebleau).

Henri II (1547–1559): the Renaissance becomes *classic* (the Louvre and the Tuileries).

The decisive turning point in French Renaissance occurred during the reign of François I. Before 1525, the artistic centre of France had been along the banks of the Loire. After the defeat at Pavia, the fountain of Renaissance art shifted toward the valley of the Seine.

Château d'Amboise (1492–1498), early Renaissance. Italian influence can be seen in the decoration but not in the construction, which remains typically French (above, top).

Château de Chenonceaux (1515–1576). Philibert Delorme's gallery over the Cher River (completed in 1576) is in striking contrast to the square main body of the castle (above).

Château de Chambord (started 1519). While its round towers are feudal, its façade, terrace, decorative details and roof are all in the Renaissance style (above).

Château de Fontainebleau. Rebuilt at the order of François I on the site of a medieval building, it has a freedom and lack of symmetry that make it typically French (below).

the Renaissance begins

Campaigning in Italy, Charles VIII was astounded by the complex polychromed facade of the charterhouse of Pavia, which bore no relation to its Gothic interior. The same of course applies to many Italian buildings of the Renaissance—interior and exterior just do not match. Although charmed, French logic could not overlook the discrepancy between outside and inside, and the French resisted the seductive southern influence.

Later France would admit the need for new exterior decoration but she did not want to sweep away the old overnight. When Charles returned to Amboise he brought with him a contingent of Italian artists who managed to change the castle utterly without so much as touching the exterior. Thus Amboise remains a French château with Italian decor. Only one architectural novelty was added: two large towers, one with a broad circular ramp up which a mounted horseman could climb.

the Renaissance takes hold

Though Italian decoration became the rage, French resistance continued: it took the form of combining brick and stone—a typical French practice, the continued use of steep roofs, rooms vaulted in the Gothic style and the arrangement of rooms around a central court. Furthermore different levels were joined by spiral staircases, often built into separate towers jutting away from the facades.

The upper part of these buildings bore imported ornamentation consisting of endless foliated scrollwork, medallions and acanthus leaves. The Italian influence also showed itself in such important contributions as arcaded galleries or loggias, caisson ceilings and, above all, pleasure gardens.

The Louis XII wing at Blois, finished in 1509, completed the complex of what was to become the first of great royal residences.

high point of the Renaissance

Stone soon supplanted the old stone-and-brick combination. Structural hangovers from medieval times such as pointed roofs, dormer windows, spiral stairways and corner towers persisted, but the Italian influence kept gaining ground.

Plan of the Château de Chambord. All the elements of a fortress are still apparent.

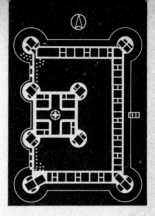

Thus at Blois the outer facade of the Francois I wing (1515–1524) introduced Bramante's rhythmical bays, and the staircase opens onto the courtyard like a porch. All the elements of a medieval fortress are lumped together at Chambord: the concordance of plan and facade, the winding staircase, the corner towers and even a moat. However the balanced symmetry of facade and the terraced roof over the central part, with its classical features, are strictly Italian in origin.

Novel changes appeared at Chenonceaux and Azay-le-Rideau: the spiral staircase lost out to one with two parallel ramps. The Italian influence also infiltrated Saint-Germain-en-Laye, started in 1539 by Pierre Chambiges. Except for the chapel, it has a terraced roof throughout, a great innovation in France (see page 23). Nonetheless the general plan is entirely French in conception.

At the Louvre, however, Pierre Lescot, in building the southwest corner of the Cour Carreé, finally made the break with the spirit of the Middle Ages.

classical Renaissance

A trio of French architects are associated with the reign of Henri II: Pierre Lescot, Philibert Delorme and Jean Bullant. Rejecting Italian trends, they tried to contact the ancient world directly instead of through Florence and Rome.

Then there were sculptors Jean Goujon and Germain Pilon, who collaborated on the decor of the Louvre's Cour Carreé, where Lescot had already provided beautifully superimposed orders and a grand staircase with straight ramps. Using antiquity as a model, Delorme attempted a valid French architectural order in the creation of columns whose drums were alternately carved and fluted. Delorme also

149

sired the château of Anet, whose monumental portal is a fine example of three superimposed orders, as well as the palace of the Tuileries, unfortunately burnt by the Commune in 1871.

Bullant, who succeeded Delorme at the Tuileries and built the château of Ecouen in his own right, used exact replicas of the ancient architectural orders.

palace of Fontainebleau

King François I commissioned

Gilles Le Breton with the construction of a palace at Fontainebleau, a palace which was duly enlarged during many succeeding reigns.

It is typically French, but the apparent symmetry of its elements is only a trompe l'oeil caused by balanced masses. The facade on the court of honor, for instance, is quite lopsided. One of the most notable features of Fontainebleau is its tall, steeply sloped slate roofs, traditional in French architecture. Another characteristic is the striking difference between its

Château de Fontaine-Henry (Calvados). High slate roofs are French, decoration Italian.

Beaugency: the city hall (1526). Despite its ornate facade, it is still in the medieval tradition.

sober exterior and highly luxuriant interior. The Italian contribution was confined to the decoration, whose exuberant detail is best displayed in the François I and Henri II galleries. The advent of the gallery, as a showpiece for the reigning monarch's glory, ushered in a dazzling trend which has extended almost to the present day and includes such masterpieces as the Stag and Diana galleries at Fontainebleau, the gallery at Chenonceaux, the gallery of Apollo in the Louvre, the famous Hall of Mirrors at Versailles, the Conference Hall at the Luxembourg and the foyer of the Paris opera.

other civil construction

Royal or noble palaces were not the only buildings going up in France at this time. Country châteaux abounded, and mansions, town and manor houses bear witness to what extent Italian decoration had been applied to traditional French structures.

The 16th century, too, brought forth remarkable town houses. The Hotel de Bourgtheroulde in Rouen is covered with superb bas-reliefs, and in Toulouse the facade of the brick Hotel d'Assézat illustrates the superimposition of the three antique orders. It

Toulouse, the Hôtel d'Assézat (1558). A superimposition of the antique orders has been applied to the courtyard facades.

was the work of Nicolas Bachelier.

As a rule, Renaissance houses kept their medieval structure but had their facades ornately decorated. Among the most resplendent buildings of this period are: the city halls of Arras, Orleans, Beaugency and Compiègne; the hospitals of Angoulême and Saint-Laurent-les-Vignes in Toulouse; the Cordouan lighthouse and the bridges of Châtellerault and Paris' Pont Neuf, which was started by Androuet du Cerceau.

religious architecture

Concentrating almost exclusively on dwellings of one sort or another, the French Renaissance left scant religious monuments. Ogival art especially persisted in this domain, Renaissance spirit only appearing in such details as the rood screen in Paris' Saint Etienne du Mont.

The foremost religious work of this period was Saint Eustache, started in 1532 in the market quarter of Les Halles. This Gothic structure relates to Notre Dame but Renaissance appears in its round arches, the superimposition of orders, and fluted pilasters with ancient capitals.

The church of Gisors, destroyed in 1940, showed an even greater change, but the new spirit only truly shines forth in Delorme's chapel for the castle of Anet, which is crowned by a caissoned dome.

Brittany at this period originated a form all its own. Complicated parish enclosures encircled the church and included an ossuary, triumphal arch and calvary. Carved from local granite, these impressive Calvary scenes sometimes included a hundred figures. The calvary of Saint Thégonnec is among the finest.

Paris: Saint Eustache (1532–1637), keystone in the choir. Although Gothic in plan, like most of the period's churches, the building has Renaissance decoration.

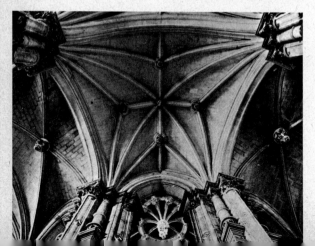

THE RENAISSANCE
IN SPAIN AND PORTUGAL

Spain

Spain's favorite Renaissance style, known as *Isabellan* or *Plateresque*, clearly derived from three conflicting trends: Gothic, Italian Renaissance and the Arab Mudejar style.

During the first half of the century, facades bore fanciful decorations which gave the architecture its name of Plateresque, from *platero*, the Spanish for goldsmith. To this period belong Enrique de Egas' University of

Salamanca, San Gregorio de Valladolid and Diego de Riaño's city hall in Seville (1528).

Religious emblems such as Saint James' scallop shell were frequently utilised for ornamental details, and in-

---

The Escorial. This palace-monastery was built near Madrid by Juan Bautista de Toledo between 1563 and 1584. Its austerity is in striking contrast to most Spanish architecture of the early 16th century.

153

deed one of Salamanca's buildings is even called the Casa de las Conchas. *Cimborios*, or lantern towers, on the other hand, were beautified with motifs taken from the Mudejar tradition. Cloisters like that of San Juan de los Reyes in Toledo were often given a plethora of opulent embellishment.

Theatrical effects were constantly in demand for the performance of rites, festivals and processions. The stairway in Burgos cathedral is typical. While Gothic tradition lingered, the spirit of the Italian Renaissance scored above all in decoration before triumphing in architecture itself.

Under the reign of Charles V and still later under Philip II, Italian influence soon outdistanced the Mudejar tradition; an example of this trend in Spanish Renaissance can be seen in the Escorial where Vignola's influence is strongly felt. Built for Philip II as a combined palace, monastery and tomb, the Escorial (1563–1584) was the brainchild of Juan Bautista de Toledo and later Juan de Herrera. This complex building with its seventeen courtyards has a 656-foot facade completely devoid of any decoration— a rarity anywhere in the world

Salamanca: Casa de Conchas. Highly decorated facades typified *plateresque* style in early Spanish Renaissance. Saint James' scallop shells were often used.

at that time and particularly astonishing in Spain.

Yet unyielding severity, harshly contrasting with the lush decoration of preceding eras, became the norm for Spanish architecture during the second half of the 16th century and the first part of the next. Madrid's Plaza Mayor (1619), the cathedral of Valladolid, also the work of Herrera, and the Lonja in Seville (1583) all have plain, austere facades.

Portugal

Spain's Isabellan style was matched by Portugal's *Manueline*. Because of its far-flung conquests and discoveries, Portugal caught the fever to build and decorate, and did so in a naturalistic, all-encompassing hybrid manner which sweepingly included elements from India as well as motifs gleaned from tropical flora and marine life. A good example of this picturesque work is the curious window from the convent of Christos de Tomar (1520).

Still experimenting, Portuguese architects and sculptors next jumbled this vegetable oddity with Moorish elements or ideas smacking of late Gothic. Moorish ideas lived on also in the use of glazed tile on outside walls.

Bizarre examples of Manueline art exist in Portugal's abbeys, particularly at Batalha, where the country's rulers lie entombed. Here towers which were to crown the chapels remain half-finished, cruelly cut off in mid-air. Later, a degree of Italian classicism came into play, and while the cloister of the Hieronymite monastery in Belém retains its ornate decoration, facades have sobered down to a restrained elegance. The dignified facade of the cloister of John III in Tomar, for instance, is already in a truly classical style. Italian influence became dominant, and the great renovator of Portuguese architecture at the end of the 16th century was Italian—Filippo Terzi, creator of the church of São Vicente in Lisbon.

Tomar: window of the Convent of Christ (1520). The *Manueline* style used a hybrid decoration whose elements derived mostly from tropical and marine fauna and flora.

THE RENAISSANCE IN GREAT BRITAIN

While Italian influence ran riot all over Europe during the 16th century, Britain remained aloof from the main cultural currents and persisted with its peculiar brand of Gothic.

On the whole, building techniques preserved the status quo and the Renaissance appeared only in decoration and sculpture. In religious architecture, a new wave could only be felt in the *chantry chapels* of the cathedrals of Salisbury, Ely and Winchester.

Nevertheless a slight evolution can be seen in civil buildings which had rhythmical facades pierced by high windows and a monumental entrance. One of Elizabeth I's architects applied an Italian trick he had picked up at Longleat (1568), where the orders are superimposed just as they are at Burghley House (1585), whose style derives from the French architect, Philibert Delorme.

Buildings like this are considered transitional between medieval and those Palladian buildings which were introduced to England by Inigo Jones at the beginning of the 17th century.

Longleat House (started 1568). Its rhythmical facade and tall windows show the slight development that took place in domestic architecture. The Renaissance had little grip in Great Britain.

THE RENAISSANCE IN NORTHERN EUROPE

In Northern Europe, particularly in Germany and the Netherlands, ogival art continued unabated for a long time. Nevertheless, even the most obdurate could not resist the new wave forever, and so we find here a blend of Gothic throwbacks and hints of Renaissance imports from France and Italy.

Structures remained more or less traditional, though some northern architects showed a marked preference for Italian decoration of a generally excessive character.

the Low Countries

The Flemish applied intricately carved decoration to ogival structure to create a style known as *Baroque Gothic.* Facades, windows and gables were all covered with profusely ornate sculpture. The Bruges city hall (1520) best typifies this period when Renaissance ideas were superimposed on late Gothic structures without a jot of concern for artistic balance. The composite style was also common and the palace of

Brussels: the guild houses. The Flemish applied ornate Renaissance decoration to basically ogival structures, thus creating "Baroque Gothic".

the prince-bishops of Liège (1526) could boast of both a colonnaded courtyard and Gothic windows.

The end of this evolution can be seen in the city hall of Antwerp (1561-1565), the work of Cornelis Floris. Here French influence far outweighs Italian. In the middle of a rather sober two-story fa-

157

Antwerp: city hall (1561–1565). French influence predominates in this structure, which illustrates a fusion of Renaissance ideas with local traditions.

Munich, Saint Michael (1583–1597). This Jesuit church, largest of the Counter-Reformation period, shows the trend that would dominate the following century.

cade, a projecting part with columns is surmounted by a Gothic-inspired gable. The unity of the whole proves that Renaissance concepts can fuse amicably with local custom to form a new and individual style.

The same sort of development may be seen in the smaller-scaled, brick city hall of The Hague (1564–1565).

During this prosperous period, city halls, commercial buildings and courthouses mushroomed across the land. The extravagance of their opulently decorated interiors is now called *Renaissance Baroque*. In front of the city halls, vast squares were surrounded by guildhalls with fantastically worked wrought-iron grills. Perhaps the most gorgeous of all these great squares is the Grande Place in Brussels.

Germany

In Germany wooden construction still reigned supreme, and, as in France, architecture remained outwardly Gothic but with Italianate decoration. The Peller house in Nuremburg, the castles of Brieg in Silesia and Wismar in Mecklenburg, as well as the city hall of Leipzig (1556), belong to this period. We must also mention the first of the German Baroque churches, Saint Michael of Munich (1583–1597), which shows that the new spirit had indeed penetrated the north.

Generally speaking, civil architecture predominated, and the Renaissance spirit was felt soonest in southern Germany, particularly in Augsburg.

Czechoslovakia

In the central and northern European countries farthest from the source of the Renaissance, Italian influence arrived late and with less impact.

In Czechoslovakia, however, Italian art had been purely and simply tacked on to Ferdinand I's Belvedere castle in Prague (1536). Slightly later, at the start of the 17th century, the same spirit repeated itself in the lodge of the Valdstejn palace. The city of Telc is also remarkable for its square surrounded by buildings crowned with Baroque gables (1530).

Telc, Czechoslovakia. This quaint square (1530) is surrounded by houses with Baroque gables. Renaissance ideals touched Central Europe only lightly.

CLASSIC AND BAROQUE

classic architecture

In speaking of *classical architecture*, we mean the trend which started with Philibert Delorme at the end of the French Renaissance and continued into the 17th century under the guidance of François Mansart. Inspired by Graeco-Roman forms, this type of architecture was based on the use of the antique orders, a careful balancing of volumes and the proportions of component parts. Thus it opposed both Baroque and Romanticism. François Mansart's Château de Maisons at Saint Germain-en-Laye, with its superimposition of the three orders, and Jules Hardouin-Mansart's Place Vendôme in Paris, with Corinthian columns, typify classic architecture (see pages 165 and 162).

baroque architecture

Baroque architecture was born of Rome's 16th century Counter-Reformation; then expanded during the next hundred years to inundate Italy, Bohemia, Austria, Germany, and Spain and its American colonies—before degenerating into Rococo in the 18th century. Orders are colossal, curves and counter-curves dominate and volumes are offset. Buildings were also characterised by the richness of the materials used, often polychrome, and by abundance of decoration and the triumph of trompe l'oeuil. Bernini's portico for Saint Peter's in Rome and Borromini's church of San Carlo alle Quattro Fontane (page 187) are typical Baroque structures.

Paris: dome of the Invalides (1679–1706). Here Jules Hardouin-Mansart beautifully illustrated the tenets of classical architecture: balanced volumes, ideal proportions and the use of the antique orders.

Rome: west facade and dome of Saint Peter's. Effect is achieved here through exaggerated proportions. Note the colossal pilasters around the drum and many offsets.

TRANSITION BETWEEN RENAISSANCE AND CLASSICISM

The Renaissance eventually ended in anarchy. By the time peace had returned, a brand new architecture had been born—a reaction against the previous century's Italian influence. In France, this new fashion corresponded with the reigns of Henri IV and Louis XIII. It employed bricks and stone together; a simplicity and harmony of plans and volumes; and elegant decoration fastidiously placed onto regular but subdued facades for accent.

This too was the era of great royal squares, an early kind of city planning centered on the statue of the reigning king. The triangular Place Dauphine in Paris was started in 1605, while the Place des Vosges, formerly the Place Royale (1612), was laid out on a square plan.

Henri IV kept up the good work on the Louvre and at Fontainebleau, and Marie de Medici engaged Salomon de Brosse to build the Luxem-

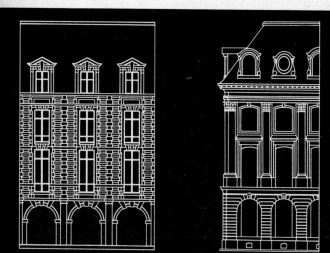

bourg Palace. De Brosse also created the great hall in the law courts and designed Rennes' city hall.

Whole new cities were constructed, among them Charleville, Henrichemont and especially Richelieu, where Lemercier's castle follows Jansenist thinking in rejecting all ornamentation. This transitional period also saw the construction of the castles of Vizille and Cadillac, the lovely town houses of Montescot in Chartres and Sully in Paris and the city hall of La Rochelle, as well as Louis XIII's hunting lodge at Versailles, the core of his son's later and grander palace.

Under the sway of the Counter-Reformation the Jesuit style predominated in religious architecture. Paris' church of Saint Gervais-Saint Protais (1616) is a near-perfect example; its facade with three superimposed orders was widely imitated. Lemercier's chapel for the Sorbonne (1642) was one of the first French churches to crown the crossing of its transept with a lantern and dome.

Left to right: Paris—the regular facades of the Place Royale (1612), now Place des Vosges, and the Place Vendôme (1698). Chartres—a wing of the Hôtel de Montescot (1614). Versailles—detail of the central building overlooking the gardens (1678).

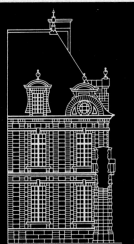
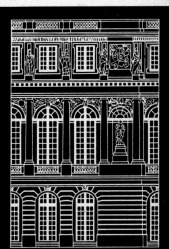

FRENCH CLASSICAL ARCHITECTURE OF THE 17TH CENTURY

The golden reign of French architecture—a veritable treasure house of gems—deserves full comment. It began in 1634 under Richelieu (d. 1642), continued under Mazarin (d. 1661), and ended with Louis XIV's death in 1715. The writer Charles Perrault called it alternately the "Great Century" or "the Century of Louis the Great," and it must be agreed that the Sun King, with his 72-year reign, easily dominated the age.

Weary of Italian Renaissance ornate fantasies, French architects tried to create an entirely national style that severed all connection with Rome. French art thus gave Europe a classicism which in the end triumphed over both the Baroque of Italy and Spain and the Realism of the Flemish and Dutch.

In the 17th century, Paris and indeed all of France acquired a fresh look. Classicism hinting of a distant past became the rage. As the new capital went up at Versailles, Paris grew overnight, as it were, with domes

everywhere; and a rash of porticos—either with Ionic or Corinthian columns—were added to churches. This was also the age of gargantuan châteaux with formal parks and what later became known as French-style gardens. In cities, meticulously laid out squares and triumphal arched gateways honored the King.

Richelieu and Mazarin (1634–1661)

François Mansart. The first of the Mansart dynasty of architects stubbornly refused to go to Italy. He sired the Château de Maisons (today Maisons-Laffitte) and the castle at Balleroy; the town houses, or "hôtels," of Toulouse, de la Vrillière and Aumont; and the church of Val-de-Grâce in Paris.

Louis Le Vau. Appointed the king's first architect in 1654, he was the key man of the transitional epoch. He built the Hôtel Lambert and the Hôtel de Lauzun in Paris. He also built the famous castle of Vaux-le-Vicomte where he

Château de Maisons (1642), by François Mansart, paved the way for classical architecture. The single building has a main body and two short wings.

Collège des Quatre-Nations (1688), now the French Academy, Paris. A certain Italian Baroque influence can be felt in this fine work by Le Vau.

collaborated for the first time with the painter Le Brun and the landscape architect Le Nôtre, both of whom were to rejoin him later at Versailles. In 1661 he laid down the plans for the Collège des Quatre-Nations, today the French Institute where the forty "immortals" sit. A certain amount of Italian in-fluence touched by Baroque can be seen in his work: colossal orders, curves, counter-curves and rather ponderous decorative elements.

At the death of Mazarin in 1661 the king faced two warring camps: emerging monumental classicism and Baroque decoration.

the Sun King
1661–1690

Together, Louis XIV and Jean Baptiste Colbert established a centralised system for the arts. Named superintendent of building, Colbert was able to discipline the two opposing tendencies to create French classicism; and the French Academy in Rome was founded to serve as a training school where prospective state artists could make an analytical study of antiquity.

Louis Le Vau worked at Versailles from 1663 to 1670.

The Louvre, the colonnade (1678), built according to the plans of d'Orbay.

Versailles: the chapel (1699–1710). This work of Hardouin-Mansart and de Cotte was treated in the classical manner of contemporary churches.

His partner François d'Orbay further extended classicism after a sojourn in Rome.

Jules Hardouin-Mansart succeeded Le Vau in 1678 and upon Colbert's death in 1683 became first architect to the king. He gaily catered to the king's building whims without a thought of the staggering expenses involved. Hardouin-Mansart was responsible for that part of the Versailles palace facing the gardens; the Grand Trianon, Place Vendôme and the Place des Victoires in Paris; and the dome of the Invalides, perhaps the century's finest piece of work.

The return to antiquity. The use of antique orders became positively mandatory and architects devoutly referred back to the works of Palladio, Scamozzi, Vignola and Serlio. Thus during the reign of Louis XIV there was a pronounced antique revival, though huge roofs still dominated the buildings. The few exceptions were the colonnade of the Louvre, the garden facade of Versailles and the Grand Trianon.

art becomes freer (1690–1715)

Le Brun's death in 1690, following Colbert's by only a few years, put an end to the state domination of art. The treasury was empty and the building budget cut by 80%. The gardens at Versailles were very slowly completed. Work at Trianon, Marly and Meudon was pushed ahead on a smaller scale.

Servile copies of antique began to be supplanted by artists giving free rein to their expression—thus announcing the advent of the 18th century.

Plans of the Château de Maisons (1642) and Vaux-le-Vicomte (below; 1661). In the latter Le Vau reduced the wings to simple forebuildings.

The king ordered the construction of a chapel for Versailles, which Jules Hardouin-Mansart covered with a very tall slate roof. When Hardouin-Mansart died in 1708 his brother-in-law Robert de Cotte liberated Versailles architecture another degree. Furthermore his nephew Jacques-Ange Gabriel became Louis XV's architect.

castles

The "Great Century" spawned scores of classical châteaux of which Versailles, naturally, heads the list.

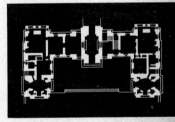

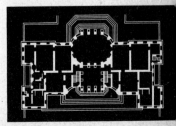

The Château de Maisons (1642) showed the trend—a simple nobility—toward classicism. Spacious lawns surround this building, which forms a single block with two short wings on each side. Instead of the customary entrance gate, an open grill enables the entire facade to be viewed from a great distance.

At Vaux-le-Vicomte the castle is even more compact, the wings appearing as mere projections. The castles of Clagny, Saint-Cloud, Meudon and Marly (J. Hardouin-Mansart) all date from this same period. Marly, the only royal residence entirely designed and completed during the reign of Louis XIV has unfortunately been destroyed.

In most castles, the main body projects only slightly and is marked simply by a pediment. Sometimes, however, as in Vaux-le-Vicomte, it turns into a semicircular projection decorated with pilasters. This arrangement was often repeated in the 18th century.

The Louvre also expanded at this time. Le Vau finished the Cour Carreé. The sumptuous colonnade, long attributed to Claude Perrault, now seems to have been the work of François d'Orbay.

the palace of Versailles

The 17th century is dominated by Versailles, the stone symbol of the French monarchy at its most dizzying pinnacle. Colbert himself selected the artists who were to work on it and Le Brun acted as technical adviser. The initial phase—a modest beginning—was simply to convert Louis XIII's old hunting lodge. Le Vau laid out the Marble Court, then "surrounded" the existing buildings to enlarge it. In the second phase, Jules Hardouin-Mansart slightly modified Le Vau's garden facade in creating the Hall of Mirrors. In order to avoid monotony in the low horizontal lines of this 250-foot-long wing, he chose an arrangement in which columns alternated with windowed arcades. He also instigated the "Mansart roofs," decorated with ornamental urns and pierced by dormers, which replaced the steep slate roofs of Le Vau. Hardouin-Mansart added two

Château de Versailles. Begun by Le Vau and continued by Hardouin-Mansart, it remains the epitome of classic architecture. Le Nôtre's park, too, shows the same majestic organisation.

500-foot wings to extend the palace on its north-south axis. He also built the Orangeries and started work on the chapel which was later completed by Robert de Cotte. He then embellished the royal housing development by adding the Grand Trianon. Mansart's genius really flowers in this airy building, a symphony of pink and green marble alternating with creamy cut stone where columns of the open peristyle connect the two flat-roofed, single-storied wings surrounding a semi-circular court.

Under the direction of Le Nôtre, the father of French gardens, the entire complex was ringed by a vast park, with gardens full of fountains and statuary.

More than thirty royal or princely residences throughout Europe drew their inspiration from Versailles and its gardens. Revealing this influence —both in distance and time —are Neumann's episcopal palace in Würzburg, San Souci in Potsdam, Schönbrunn near Vienna (p. 196), Juvara and Sachetti's La Granja near Madrid (1721), the palace of Caserta in Italy (p. 190), and Tsarskoye-Selo (1752) and Peterhof in distant Russia, as well as the Swedish Royal Palace in Stockholm. The most exact replica is the palace of Herrenchiemsee, built for Ludwig II (The Mad) of Bavaria.

royal squares and urban settings

City squares of the 17th century symbolized the royal regulatory power and represented the most illustrious examples of contemporary city planning.

Paris still has four city squares dating from this period: the Place Dauphine, the Place des Vosges, the Place des Victoires and the Place Vendôme (page 162).

The circular Place des Victoires (1686), dedicated to Louis XIV's military triumphs, was another work by Jules Hardouin-Mansart. Its buildings were set off by Ionic columns. In 1698 the same architect designed the Place Vendôme which he also dedicated to the reigning monarch. Square with cut corners, its regularly spaced bays feature arcades which are topped by Corinthian pilasters.

As the State coffers were well filled at the time, many provincial towns likewise gained attractive royal squares, all under the control of Versailles architects, whose goal was to create a national artistic pattern. Thus Tours, Pau, Caen, Dijon, Lyon, Rennes and Mont-

pellier all are blessed with handsome squares still reflecting the glory of the Sun King.

Triumphal arches and monumental gates. Aping the splendours of ancient Rome, Louis XIV commemorated his victories with such arches as Paris' Porte Saint-Martin and Port Saint-Denis as well as the gate of Vitry-le-François.

other civil and military buildings

Major works in this category include the Invalides in Paris, a work of Libéral Bruant; the Salpetrière Hospital; the city hall of Troyes; the Paris Observatory and the Pont Royal over the Seine.

Essentially functional in nature, the lines of these buildings appeared simultaneously noble and severe. The great quadrilateral of the Invalides, started by Louis XIV in 1670 to house wounded veterans, perfectly exemplifies these low horizontal buildings without projections whose majestic facades were completely devoid of useless ornamentation. The great expanse of the Invalides' facade is broken only by a monumental gate at the centre, and by two pavilions on each end.

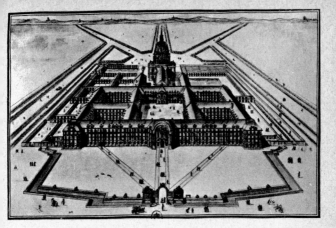

Vauban, Louis' military engineer and architect, fortified a lot of strategic cities at this same time.

Town houses. In the twilight of Louis' reign many nobles left Versailles and built themselves town houses, mostly in the Saint-Honoré and Saint-Germain quarters of Paris. Living areas were generally separated from the street by a formal court and opened onto gardens on the other side.

State apartments, usually reached by a grand staircase, were normally placed on the first or "noble" story. Rooms strung out one after another connected with symmetrically placed doors

Hôtel des Invalides, seen in perspective. It was started in 1671 by Libéral Bruant. The church was added by Hardouin-Mansart and the whole completed by de Cotte in 1708.

to accentuate the idea of stately progress. Little by little, gaudy decorative effects in these rooms gave way to the majestic simplicity of the 18th century.

The hôtels de Rohan and de Soubise, the latter now the National Archives, rose in the once fashionable Marais district, while the Faubourg Saint-Germain could boast of Boffrand's Hôtel Amelot de Gournay, Lassurance's Hôtel de Rhotelin and the Hôtel d'Estrées, whose architect was Robert de Cotte.

171

religious architecture

In the religious field architects sought new volumes, and domes became a must. Lemercier put a dome on the chapel of the Sorbonne, François Mansart put a dome on the Val-de-Grâce and the temple of Sainte Marie, and the same form capped the Collège des Quatre Nations, now the Institut. But by far the most celebrated of all was the soaring dome crowning the Invalides.

Three kinds of church plans were used concurrently: the basilical plan with aisles, ambulatory and radiating chapels, as at Saint Roch, Saint Louis-en-l'Isle and the cathedral of Versailles; a single nave without aisles but with chapels between the buttresses, as in Nôtre-Dame des Victoires in Paris; and the central plan, as at the Invalides.

Similarly there existed a choice of four types of facades: the facade framed by towers as at Saint Jacques du Haut-Pas; the facade with three superimposed orders as at Saint Paul-Saint Louis; the two-level facade with the upper story framed in volutes (such as Val-de-Grâce); and the domed facade of which the Invalides is a prototype (page 160).

Jesuit churches were gorgeously decorated (Saint Paul-Saint Louis), while their Jansenist counterparts despised any dressing up (Saint Jacques du Haut-Pas).

Saint Paul-Saint Louis Church, Paris (1641). A Jesuit-style church with a single nave and no aisles. The facade is famous for its superimposition of the three classical orders.

CLASSIC FRENCH ARCHITECTURE OF THE 18th CENTURY

The glorious and majestic 17th century was followed by the mellow and relaxed 18th—a light-hearted time of theatres and town houses, "folies," imitation temples and country pavilions. Actually, Louis XIV himself had called the turn by requesting more open and friendly structures, buildings with human warmth.

Petit Trianon (1763–1768) in Versailles, by J. A. Gabriel. Antique Corinthian columns accentuate the harmonious proportions of this tiny château.

Nevertheless, the lessons of the 17th century were kept in mind, partly due to the bond between the old and new generations of architects and partly to the lustrous status enjoyed by a form of state architecture which symbolized the cohesion and power of the monarchy. Some projects indeed resembled those of the previous century; the huge royal square in Bordeaux for instance looks very much like the Place Vendôme, while the Place de la Concorde brings to mind the colonnade of the Louvre.

Now stone was used exclusively—the beautiful French-quarried white stone which brings such distinction and gaiety to 18th century facades. Moderation, proportion and light were the ideals, and all heaviness was banished.

The first half of the century ushered in a triumph of a purely French idiom, but after 1752 a harking back to antiquity favored the development of neo-classicism. Nonetheless the biggest achievement of all this research was in laying the rock-bottom foundations of modern construction.

Antiquity's foremost spokesman was Jacques-Ange Gabriel, who shaped the revival which was to prevail in the last half of the century. Associated with him was Claude Nicolas Ledoux whose revolutionary ideas paved the way for today's architecture.

the regency (1715–1723)

Philippe d'Orléans' rule as regent during the minority of Louis XV was an era of reaction, a rejection of the absolute power wielded by Louis XIV and the overweening monumental architecture imposed on the nation by this proud sovereign.

Robert de Cotte became the state architect, taking over from his brother-in-law Mansart at Versailles. Besides his official duties, he built such private edifices as the Hôtel de Rohan in Strasbourg; the hôtels of Lude, d'Estrées and Bourbon-Conti in Paris; Bonn's Poppelsdorf castle and the castle of Brühl, plus Frankfurt's

The Chanteloup Pagoda (1778). Exoticism became the rage during the French Regency and "chinoiseries" such as this pagoda adorned parks and gardens.

174

Tour et Taxis palace (destroyed in 1944).

Jean Aubert improved on the work of his predecessor and built the Chantilly Stables as well as the remarkable Hôtel Peyrenc de Moras (1729), now the Rodin Museum in Paris.

Foreign influences ingeniously inspired originality during the Regency. China, India and Turkey being the current fashionable places, a rash of exotic decoration resulted, of which the "monkeyshines" at Chantilly and the Turkish room at the Hôtel de Rohan are prime examples. Thus the classic phase gave way to a romantic reaction that was tinged with poetic sensitivity and glamour.

Louis XV's majority (1723–1774)

Most of this century's massive architecture also marked the triumph of the Baroque curve and counter-curve. Yet the discovery in 1719 of the ruins of Herculaneum and in 1748 those of Pompeii, plus publicizing of the work at Paestum in 1764, re-kindled the classic flame which had never been entirely extinguished in French architecture. Under Louis XVI

strict classicism again took hold, and curves lost out to straight lines and triangular pediments.

Louis XVI (1774–1793)

The anti-Baroque movement had begun in 1752 with the publication of Laugier's *Essay on Architecture*. It hit its stride in the classic Petit Trianon (1763–1768) and reached full momentum under Louis XVI.

Victor Louis instigated this return to the past—a return influenced by the Italian Renaissance, as can clearly be seen in the Odéon Theatre and the courtyard of the Palais Royal.

Richard Mique now acted as the king's architect at Versailles and erected the theatre, the Temple of Love and the charming belvedere of the Petit Trianon.

city halls

The beautification campaign extended to such provincial towns as Avallon, Saulieu, Beauvais, Metz, Rennes and Toulouse; only naturally, the most care was spent on city halls strategically placed on

Strasbourg: the Rohan palace (1742). Built to Robert de Cotte's plans, it belongs to the period when the French tradition once again triumphed (above).

Chantilly: the Great Stables (1736), by Jean Aubert. The 18th century was marked by the exclusive use of stone and restrained ornamentation (below).

Place de la Concorde, Paris (1755–1775). Gabriel remembered the royal squares of the 17th century but in this case placed buildings on one side only.

Versailles: the Opéra (1770). Gabriel broke with the traditional horseshoe to build a U-shaped amphitheatre. The sculpted decoration is by Pajou.

the major municipal squares. These were generally three-story structures with a base, main floor and attic, all gracefully proportioned architecturally according to classical tenets.

Jacques-Jules Gabriel, father of Jacques-Ange Gabriel, built his epoch's best known city hall at Rennes after plans already drawn up by Salomon de Brosse.

royal squares

Louis XV kept up the royal square tradition, commissioning Jacques-Ange Gabriel to lay out the great square which bore the king's name until the revolution but is now universally famed as the Place de la Concorde. Here the innovation was to have buildings on but one side. They frame the rue Royale (1732), with its uniform buildings on either side.

A royal square was also laid out in Rennes to serve as a setting for the city hall mentioned above. It features a tall Ionic order resting on a solid lower level.

Another great square of the vintage is the one built by Jacques-Jules Gabriel in Bordeaux, with buildings on only three sides. The architect Héré planned the square in Nancy, though its magnificent cast-iron grill was created by a locksmith, Jean Lamour. This square actually consists of three elements: the Place Stanislas, the Place de la Carrière and the hemicycle—which together form a remarkable unit.

Imitations of these royal squares popped up all over Europe. Brussels' Place Royale resembles that of Reims, Lisbon's Place du Commerce is reminiscent of Bordeaux and the Amalienborg in Copenhagen seems a frank copy of the Place de la Concorde and the Place Hoche in Versailles.

theatres

In the last half of the 18th century the theatre flourished, and one of the first opera houses was Gabriel's Opéra in Versailles (1770). Its U-shaped amphitheatre represented a distinct innovation which immeasurably improved visibility and acoustics. Its grey-green and gold decor adds to the delicate appeal of the whole.

The Great Theatre of Bordeaux (1780). Adopting the mode of the day, Victor Louis surrounded the theatre with a Corinthian colonnade.

Victor Louis' masterpiece, his Bordeaux theatre, which was the first theatre built as a separate unit, had enormous reception rooms which were copied by Charles Garnier when he built the Paris Opéra. An impressive Corinthian colonnade in the current style completely encircles this theatre.

Ledoux created a lyre-shaped amphitheatre in Besançon, and for the first time the orchestra section was fitted with seats.

civil and military architecture

Paris's Ecole Militaire, another of Jacques-Ange Gabriel's major works, remains unrivalled both for its overall design and the attention lavished on detail. As for the School of Surgery in Gondoin (started in 1766) we again find all the fashionable antique trappings: a triumphal arch and an operating amphitheatre built like a Roman theatre, complete with such features as tiered seats and vomitoria.

Houses. The 18th century was a golden age for private dwellings. After the death of Louis XIV the nobles could and did move back to Paris, and their return led to the construction of many vast and comfortable town houses. Architecture was once more brought down to human scale and the resulting residences became in general more intimate, cozy and practical.

Rooms were connected by corridors rather than running one into another; and large reception salons, often oval, looked out on stylised gardens. Beams and joists vanished from sight and private apartments kept quite aloof from reception rooms. Each apartment consisted of a bedroom, antechamber, wardrobe and bathroom or, as this part of the unit was then called, "the conveniences."

Town houses. The Hôtel de Peyrenc de Moras, a happy product of the partnership of Jean Aubert and Jacques-Jules Gabriel, is noted for its simplicity of line, the easy convenience of its floor plan and its exquisitely designed gardens.

Not one town house of this period is mediocre, and most of the Paris ones are ministries today, e.g., Villeroy, Matignon, Bourbon, de Roquelaure and Charost. The Hôtel d'Evreux now lodges the President of France. The Hôtel de Soubise, with its fabulous decor by Boffrand, contains the National Archives. Rousseau's Hôtel de Salm, currently the chancellery of the Legion of Honor, is distinguished by its simplicity and balance as well as for its elegant entrance porch.

Castles. One of the finest buildings erected toward the close of Louis XV's reign is the Petit Trianon at Versailles. This soberly elegant royal residence was built by J.-A. Gabriel at Madame de Pompadour's behest (1763–1768). Its columns and perfectly composed square plan vividly attest to its classical heritage.

Back in 1751 the same architect started the castle of Compiègne, a compact structure contrasting with the

rambling layout of Fontaine-bleau or Versailles.

The "folies." This was also the day when pretty little pleasure domes were erected here and there in Paris suburbs to give city dwellers an excuse for getting a breath of fresh air. Perhaps most typical of these "folies" is the Casino de Bagatelle, built for the Comte d'Artois in a mere ninety days by Bélanger.

Versailles Cathedral (1754), by Mansart de Sagonne. Plan is traditional; elevation is classical. Only the bulbous towers reflect the new taste.

Hôtel Peyrenc de Moras (1729), Paris, by Aubert and Gabriel, a typical work with simple lines and discreet sculpted ornamentation.

religious architecture

During this period few religious structures were built. The major exceptions were J.-A. Gabriel's cathedral of La Rochelle (1741) and Mansart's cathedral of Versailles and the church of Sagonne (1743–1754), whose bulbous towers hint of Baroque.

The classic trend reappeared with Saint Sulpice in Paris. A design competition in 1731 was won by Servandoni with a plan calling for two-story towers and porticos on the same facade.

Soufflot's Panthéon, whose cornerstone was laid in 1751, assumed the shape of a Greek cross each of whose arms is divided into three naves. Its facade imitates an antique temple, with columns topped by a triangular pediment. Above the whole rises a huge dome set on a drum surrounded by a colonnade. This building is inseparable from its setting, and the square facing it was also designed by Soufflot.

Two other Parisian churches show the return to the antique mode: Chalgrin's Saint Philippe-du-Roule (1774) and Brongniart's Capucin convent.

Claude Nicolas Ledoux

Dubbed "the mad architect," Ledoux was in fact a forerunner of modern architecture. His classical side produced such buildings as the castle of Eaubonne, the du Barry pavilion at Louveciennes, the castle of Bénouville and the theatre of Besançon. The opposite side of the coin, his fantasy, resulted in such wonders as the royal salt works at Arc-et-Senans and the Maupertuis factory with its spherical house, as well as the Paris toll houses, the Rotunda in the Parc Monceau, the gate houses on the Avenue d'Orléans and the Place du Trône, the Rotunda in suburban La Villette.

His greatest feat was perhaps his design for an ideal integrated city, Chaux, in which function would dictate form. "We can make epic poems and elegies from the circle and square," he said. "In a factory round and square pillars are much more suitable than any of the known orders."

The construction Ledoux left unfinished hints at his sad story. Fired from office in 1789 and thrown into prison, he thereupon wrote a tome: *On architecture, considered in its relation to art, customs and legislation.* Barely escaping the guillotine, he was forbidden to continue his work and could not even, by 1797, collect his fees for designing the gates of Paris.

The Revolution delivered French architecture a knockout blow and ended once and for all its position as world champion. Nevertheless, the seeds of modern architecture had been sown.

Director's House of La Loue. Simultaneously classical and romantic, Claude Nicolas Ledoux's work foreshadowed modern architecture.

EUROPEAN BAROQUE
OF THE 17TH AND 18TH CENTURIES

As we have already noted, Baroque opposed classicism (see CLASSIC AND BAROQUE ARCHITECTURE, page 160). It is also apparent that the Renaissance lingered on for many years in some countries, so that fixing arbitrary limits to one period or another is extremely difficult, particu-

larly as arts of different countries do not always develop along parallel lines.

At the same time that classic architecture was prospering in France during the 17th century, classicism's opposite, Baroque, flourished in Italy, Germany, Bohemia and Austria, before finally being tempered in the 18th century by the far-reaching influence of Versailles (which eventually touched even Russia).

Saint Peter's Square, Rome (1629–1667), the work of Bernini. Four rows of Doric columns enclose this great oval whose major axis measures 1,115 feet.

183

ITALIAN BAROQUE—AN EXTENSION
OF THE RENAISSANCE

Baroque was an offspring of the Mannerism which Rome embraced after 1550. Carlo Maderna could be considered its originator, since the facade of his church of Santa Susanna in Rome (1623) already anticipates Baroque. The movement reached its climax between 1625 and 1675 under Bernini, Pietro da Cortona and Borromini. There were no large-scale projects going on but rather a series of small churches with short lines and undulating curves. These include San Andrea al Quirinale in Rome (completed in 1671) and, near Rome, Santa Maria della Assuntione in Arricia and San Tomas de Villanova in Castel Gondolfo, all three by Bernini. In addition to San Luca and Santa Marta (1650), the first church with a bulging facade and pilasters, Pietro da Cortona built Santa Maria della Pace (1657) and Santa Maria Via Lata (1663), both of whose facades are fairly restrained.

San Carlo alle Quattro Fontane (1638–1667), also known as the Carlino (page

San Andrea al Quirinale, Rome (1671). A typical Baroque church by Bernini, with its oval plan, curved walls and pilastered facade (left).

Venice: Santa Maria della Salute (1631–1685), Longhena's masterpiece. Enormous inverted scrolls link the dome to the aisles (right).

187), grandly illustrates Borromini's ornate style with its complex floor plan and the combination of convex and concave volumes of its facade.

Saint' Ivo alla Sapienza (1650) and Sant' Agnese (1657) also belong to Borromini, who has been called the inventor of Rococo. Such architecture, the most tortuous and artificial in existence, was to conquer a huge audience in Europe. The interplay of offset pediments on the facade of Martino Longhi's San Vincenzo-Sant' Anastasio well typifies Baroque excess.

Sant' Ignazio, constructed according to the plans of the Dominican Grassi, represents

an even more Baroque version of the Gesu. It was the largest Roman church the Jesuits built on this plan.

Baroque meant facades covered with ornamentation, and lavish interiors whose decorative effects depended much on sculpture. Its high priest, Bernini, creator of the awesome bronze canopy over the high altar of Saint Peter's, as well as the statue, "Ecstasy of Saint Theresa," was an architect as well as sculptor. His most gorgeous

work remains the 1,115-ft. oval of Saint Peter's Square (1629–1667) with its quadruple Doric colonnade. (It was finally completed by Carlo Fontana who added its trapezoidal court.) Bernini also created the Scala Regia, or Stairway of Honour, of the Vatican, a jewel of perspective.

In Venice, where the traditions of the previous century still held strong, Longhena erected his masterpiece, the church of Santa Maria della Salute (1631–1685). At a time when most church architecture followed the lead of the Gesu, its massive dome—braced by enormous inverted consoles—and its plan with an ambulatory and chapels are especially original. Longhena also built the exquisitely proportioned Rezzonico Palace and the freer and more ornate Pesaro Palace. Both date from 1650 and both face the Grand Canal. The same period saw the building of Benoni's Dogana di Mare (1682).

Elsewhere in northern Italy—in Turin—Guarino Guarini, an Oratorian monk and disciple of Borromini, distinguished himself by building San Lorenzo (1687), whose plan combines a square with an octagon. Its dome is supported by an eight-cornered star of ribs, a design perhaps borrowed from the

great mosque of Córdoba. Guarini's Carignano Palace of 1680 has a facade which undulates in a concave-convex-concave curve.

Guarini—who designed churches for foreign cities like Prague—and his colleague Borromini can be considered the inventors of German Baroque, and their influence was decisive throughout central Europe.

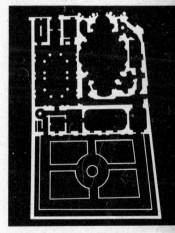

Rome: San Carlo alle Quattro Fontane (1638–1667) by Borromini. The movement of Baroque architecture can be seen here in the complexity of concave and convex volumes which create curves and counter-curves on the facade. The *entablature*, too, follows every curve in the building.

ITALIAN BAROQUE IN THE 18TH CENTURY

Rome went in for spectacular effects in the 18th century, and this theatricality produced such grandiose landmarks as Francesco de Sanctis' stairs on the Piazza di Spagna (1725); Nicolas Salvi's Trevi Fountain (1762), a real triumphal arch plastered onto the facade of a palace; Ferdinand Fuga's facade for Santa Maria Maggiore (1743), and Alessandro Galilei's copious work on San Giovanni in Laterano (St. John Lateran), which consisted of a double portico

flanked by a monumental order and crowned with a balustrade surmounted by statues (1735).

In Turin, Filippo Juvara, a student of Fontana, built the basilica of Superga, begun in 1717, but unfortunately the dome, portico and campanile are ill-assorted. A thank offering for Turin's liberation in 1706, this building sparks interest because of its construction in reverse: the dome and apse are on the facade.

From 1729 to 1733 the same architect built the Stupinigi Palace, residence of the dukes of Savoy and kings of Sardinia. In this building, double wings approach and retreat from one another to

Rome: the Trevi Fountain (1762), by Nicolas Salvi. Roman artists of the 18th century sought spectacular effects such as that produced by this monumental fountain.

Rome: Saint John Lateran (1735). Alessandro Galilei obtained theatrical results in this church, with its porticoed facade surmounted by statues.

Turin: the basilica of Superga (begun 1717) by Filippo Juvara. Dome and apse are on the facade, though the whole never strays far from the classic ideal.

form three successive courtyards, while the whole is dominated by a vast three-story salon cut by interior balconies—a perfect setting for the trompe l'oeil paintings so popular at the time. The painter Tiepolo excelled in this art, his best work appearing in the Villa Pisani of Stra in the Veneto, now known as the Villa Nazionale.

Versailles inspired still another building: the Royal Palace of Caserta, started in 1752

by Luigi Vanvitelli for Charles III of Naples, who yearned to keep up with his Bourbon cousin. Caserta, completed in 1774, forms a square (656 feet on each side) with a five-story facade and terraced roof. The colonnaded fore-buildings, chapel and park look rather like French work of the time, but the decoration is opulently Baroque. In sheer exuberance, though, it does not surpass the Capodimonte castle near Naples built in 1738 by Medrano, which has a hamlet resembling Marie Antoinette's bucolic plaything at the Trianon.

The Baroque spirit did not stop at architecture and decor but permeated settings and backgrounds as well—in a word, gardens. Owners of country villas never ceased vying with one another in this way, and the result was such floral paradises as that of the Villa Torlonia in Frascati, famous for its waterfall; the Borghese and Doria-Pamphilii gardens in Rome, the Gamberaia gardens in Settignano and the curious flower beds of the Villa Garzoni in Collodi.

But finally the program could go no further—Italy had spent herself. The torch now passed to other countries in central and northern Europe who would seek originality through adopting Baroque ideas to their own customs and traditions.

The Royal Palace of Caserta (begun 1752). An example of Baroque classicism in which Vanvitelli took his cue from Versailles, mainly in the colonnaded forebuildings. Decor is nonetheless Baroque.

SPAIN AND PORTUGAL IN THE 17TH AND 18TH CENTURIES

In the 17th century the Spanish crown was too poor to build anything even though the church and religious orders were swollen with money, and this is why the architecture of this period is mostly ecclesiastical.

Three types of plans dominated church construction:
—The first, following Spanish traditions, had a nave and lateral chapels inscribed in a rectangle, such as Juan Gomez de Mora's collegiate church in Salamanca.
—The second was a cruciform plan with three naves dating back to ogival art; typical was the Dominican church in Seville.

—The third, central plan was Italian in origin and could be octagonal, circular or elliptical. San Lorenzo in Burgos exemplifies this type.

The severity that Juan de Herrera showed in the cathedral of Valladolid gave way to the Baroque splendour of Ordonez' Jesuit church for the college of Alcalà (1602) and de Mora's Salamanca collegiate church (1614). Soon fantasy and

Salamanca: Plaza Mayor (completed 1755). The Churrigueresque kind of Spanish Baroque features overelaborate ornamentation.

Church of San Francisco d'Acate-pec, Mexico. Spanish Baroque overflowed into Central and South America where it merged with local elements.

Queluz Castle, Portugal (1794), built by Mateus Vicente and a Frenchman, L. B. Robillon. The latter decorated the apartments and laid out gardens in the manner of Le Nôtre.

quaint conceits gained the upper hand as painters and sculptors added their arts. Polychrome tiles on the domes of the Pilar church in Saragossa by Francisco de Herrera the Younger are a case in point.

French and Italian influences can be detected in such 18th century buildings as the Royal Palace of Madrid, the work of G. B. Sacchetti (1738); while the palace of La Granja (1721–1739), near Segovia, obviously copies Versailles. Robert de Cotte himself drew up the plans for the Buen Retiro residence near Madrid (1731) and another Frenchman, Marchand, built the castle of Aranjuez (1717).

The most amazing Baroque building of all is Narciso Tomé's Toledo Cathedral (1732). Its wondrously fantastic decoration, called *churrigueresque* after architect José Churriguera, also embellishes Pedro de Ribera's portal for the Madrid hospital (1722) and the sacristy of the charterhouse of Granada (1747).

Spain subsequently turned to neo-classicism as the result of a 1777 royal edict forbidding the slightest hint of regionalism in Spanish architecture.

Latin America. Meanwhile Spanish Baroque crossed the ocean and gave Central and South America such works as the cathedrals of Mexico City, Puebla, Mérida and Michoacán. At the same time that Casas y Novoa was building the facade of Santiago de Compostela, the Churrigueresque style reached its crux in Mexico. The churches of Ocotlán, Tlaxcala, Tepotzotlán, Santo Domingo de Puebla and Santa Clara de Querétaro all were built between 1730 and 1783. A good example of Spanish Baroque may also be found in Peru at the episcopal palace of Lima.

Portugal. Following in the wake of the Italian Guarini's Church of the Divine Providence in Lisbon, the Baroque movement in Portugal assumed a native form, encouraged by the reconstruction of the Portuguese capital after the 1735 earthquake. Concave and convex arches and tall lofty facades such as those at the Mafra monastery and the Artillery Museum in Lisbon are typical of the period. A Portuguese and a Frenchman—Mateus Vicente and L. B. Robillon—designed the Royal Castle of Queluz near Lisbon; its garden facade has the look of a Gabriel building.

BAROQUE IN THE NETHERLANDS AND SCANDINAVIAN COUNTRIES

Netherlands. In 1630 the Netherlands took up the Palladian style, whose classic rigidity can be seen in Constantijn Huygens' house and in the Hague Mauritshuis. Van Campen began Amsterdam's classical city hall in 1648; later it became the Royal Palace. French influence held all civil construction in an iron grip, Baroque only appearing in religious edifices.

Toward the close of the century Dutch buildings closely resembled their English counterparts before surrendering completely to French influences. Examples are Amsterdam's Trippenhuis, the Vingboors town house of 1662, and Venekool's city hall for Enkhuisen, 1686.

Denmark was the first Scandinavian country to adopt Western architectural styles. The Dutch intervention continued from the 16th into the 17th century, appearing in the royal castles of Kronborg at Elsinore, Frederiksborg at Hillerod, and Rosenborg at Copenhagen, as well as in the Nybder houses and the Stock Exchange in Copenhagen. Stone, brick and copper were the most common building materials.

French influence took over in the 18th century with a Frenchman named superintendent of royal buildings. Nicolas-Henri Jardin built the Knights' Hall in Copenhagen's Christianborg castle, the Frederik V church with its resplendent dome, bigger even than that of the Invalides, and the royal Amalienborg square to serve as setting for Saly's statue of Frederik V.

Sweden. At mid 17th century Simon and Jean de la Vallee built the Nobles' Palace in Stockholm, and two Swedish architects, the elder and younger Tessin, followed the French line in building Drottningholm castle and Stockholm's Royal Palace.

Augsburg: city hall (1608). The Palladian influence is visible, but the bulbous towers already forecast the imminent triumph of Baroque late in the century.

CENTRAL EUROPEAN BAROQUE

In the 17th century Germanic and Italian art could hardly be distinguished as the works of such Italian architects as Canevale, Caratti and Martinelli spread like wildfire throughout central Europe.

A leavening of Palladio is quite apparent in Augsburg's city hall (1608), though its bulbous towers already foreshadow the new trend which was to appear at the end of the century. Baroque really took root thanks partly to Andreas Schlüter who used Baroque detail on the Royal Palace in Berlin (1698–1706.)

Austria, and Vienna in particular, took Baroque to its bosom. A splendid example is Fischer von Erlach's Royal Palace of Schönbrunn (1691). Erlach used a Baroque plan for Saint Charles church in Vienna (1715–1737), though the decorated columns flanking the main entrance could be considered classic elements; he also designed most of the churches in Salzburg.

The Hague: Mauritshuis, begun in 1633 by Pieter Post and Jacob van Campen. Its classic style betrays the dominating influence of Palladio, Baroque being then limited to ecclesiastical buildings.

195

Another architect, Lukas von Hildebrandt, employed both French and Italian styles. He built the palace complex of Belvedere for Prince Eugène of Savoy in a Vienna suburb between 1714 and 1721. Around this complex, prettily laid out gardens remind one of a rather quixotic Versailles.

Bavaria. Here again two schools flourish side by side: the court style inspired by the French; and the religious offshoot of Italian Baroque.

Interior of the "Wies" church in Bavaria (1754). Built by Domenikus Zimmerman, its architectural qualities are almost obliterated by the overall stucco decoration.

Vienna: The Royal Palace of Schönbrunn (1691). Fischer von Erlách, though influenced by Roman Baroque, built a palace mainly inspired by Versailles.

Amalienburg Pavilion (1739), in the Nymphenburg Palace gardens near Munich, belongs to the first group. Its author is François Cuvilliés, a pupil of François Blondel.

The second group comprises a fascinating succession of fancifully decorated churches: Johann Michel Fischer's church of Ottoburen, Domenikus Zimmerman's masterful "Wies" pilgrim church (1754), and Balthasar Neumann's Vierzehnheiligen church at Staffelstein (1744), where the isolated high altar forms the centre of the composition.

Saxony. The same duality is found in the Zwinger palace (1722) by M. D. Pöppelmann at Dresden, a dazzling piece of German Rococo, and in George Bähr's Frauen Kirche (1740) also in Dresden.

Prussia. Frederick II, the Great, ordered the construction of the Potsdam city hall (1753) along classic lines, then went on to build the castle of Sans-Souci.

Bohemia. Czechoslovak Baroque developed in three distinct phases, particularly in Prague. To the initial 17th century part belongs Saint Mary of the Victory (1613) as well as the Mathias gate on the castle towering over the city (1614). Typical of

Prague: the Czernin Palace. Here Caratti typified Czech Baroque during its Italian phase—before a national style was adopted.

the second Italianate phase are Valdstejn Palace, the Jesuit college (by Loragho), the Jesuit church of Saint Ignatius (the work of Loragho and Orsi), the Czernin Palace (Caratti).

In the third period a national Baroque style flourished. In Prague: nave of Saint Nicolas in Malá Strana by Krystof Dientzenhofer; churches of Saint John Nepomuk.

Poland. Here again, French influence prevailed in civil architecture and Baroque in religious. The church of the Holy Cross in Warsaw was built by an Italian, Fontana.

RUSSIA IN THE
17TH AND 18TH CENTURIES

In the 17th century Russia at last opened up somewhat to Western influences despite the persistence of a strong Byzantine tradition. Purely native forms also existed however, including the outside galleries on the churches of the Upper Volga, the wooden places of worship in northern Russia and the widespread use of bulbs and polychrome decoration. Oriental influence showed itself mainly in the form of floral ornamentation.

New forms and ideas were brought in, first by the Italians, then by Germans and Dutch. Poland appropriated the basilical plan and windows became larger and crowned with pediments, as on the church of the Virgin in Rostov. Baroque ornamentation made its appearance, as can be seen from the wooden palace of Kolomenskoye and the church of the prophet Elijah in Yaroslavl.

During the 18th century, Western culture took solid root. In building the new capital at St. Petersburg,

Peter the Great chose Amsterdam and Versailles as models, the latter because of its grandeur. Amsterdam's canals, quays and houses were reproduced in Saint Petersburg (now Leningrad), the work done mostly by a varied crew of French artisans. A Parisian architect, Leblond, designed the Strelman Palace as well as the castle of Peterhof and the Nevski Prospekt.

Although French influence continued throughout the century it was an Italian architect, Rastrelli, that the Empress Elizabeth commissioned to build the Winter Palace (1756–1762) and Tsarskoye-Selo, still another duplicate of Versailles. Rastrelli also designed the church of Saint Andrew in Kiev and the huge convent of Smolny, which anticipates contemporary Soviet gigantism.

In 1759 Catherine the Great ordered Vallin de La Mothe to build the Beaux Arts Academy and the Hermitage, both in Saint Petersburg. By this time even Russian architects had fixed upon western Baroque, as evidenced by Starov's Tauride Palace.

ENGLAND DURING THE 17TH AND 18TH CENTURIES

Every rule must have an exception, and England was just that in her utter disdain of Italian Baroque and German Rococo and her steadfast loyalty to Palladio. Inigo Jones' Queen's House in Greenwich (1616) set the fashion for neo-classicism. It was a true Italian villa complete with loggia, though with a rather surprisingly barren exterior.

A few years later, the columns and pediment of the Banquetting Hall in Whitehall (1621) and the Ionic orders of Lindsey House in London's Lincoln's Inn Fields revealed the full glory of the Renaissance to the English. Actually, private construction at that time was partially subject to Renaissance influences and partly to Dutch trends, while monumental architecture took its cue from the French as well.

Sir Christopher Wren's work shows that he was not immune to French encitement. After the Great Fire of London in 1666, Wren drew up the plans for fifty-one churches. He rebuilt Saint Paul's with a Greek cross design (1675–1710), at about the same time that Mansart was erecting the Invalides (1670–1706). Saint Paul's dome, spanning 108 feet, compares

Queen's House, Greenwich (1616). Inigo Jones brought Palladian classicism to England with this surprisingly open Italianate villa.

199

with the one on the Invalides or even to Saint Peter's in Rome.

Wren's only trip abroad was to Paris, after which, in 1685, he gave the facade of Saint Paul's double Corinthian columns like those of the Louvre colonnade. Wren also devised his own version of Baroque classicism, as witness Saint Stephen Walbrook, London.

When Baroque finally did arrive in England at the close of the 17th century, it assumed a form quite different from that on the continent. Called Romantic Baroque or Proto-romanticism, its most incisive examples are Wren's Cambridge Library, William Talman's Chatsworth House (1696), Hawksmoor and Townesend's Clarendon Library at Oxford (1714) and Blenheim Palace, started by Sir John Vanbrugh in 1705, where the lines of a Palladian villa are combined with the grandeur and scale of Versailles.

Early in the 18th century, with the advent of the Hanovers the tide turned from the Baroque of Wren, Vanbrugh and Hawksmoor toward a neo-Palladian style. Chiswick House near London (the work of Lord Burlington and William Kent, 1725) repeats the theme of Palladio's Villa Capra near Vicenza, Italy, as do Holkham Hall in Norfolk

---

Saint Paul's Cathedral, London (1675–1710). In this major work of Wren, the dome compares with that of the Invalides in Paris (p. 161) and Saint Peter's in Rome (p. 143).

and the Assembly Rooms in York (Burlington, 1730.)

This antique revival, paralleling the same movement in France, was joyfully embraced by architects James Adam and Sir William Chambers, who produced innumerable private country houses along these lines. The time was ripe. Country abodes dramatically contrasted with London dwellings which were jammed next to each other. Dutch-style housing had begun to go up in London back in the latter half of the 17th century—rectangular brick buildings with stone piers whose entrance and facade were surmounted by pediments: e.g., Fenton House in Hampstead. Now, in the 18th century, all that remained to be done was to Italianise these Dutch structures along Palladian lines by tacking on wings connected to the main building by porticos, colonnades, pediments, balustrades and broad exterior stairways. A sample of this is Prior Park near Bath, built by John Wood the Elder in 1735. This rather imitative architecture was set in an entirely original creation: the English garden. Parks and gardens were also built in cities, and Wood and his son, after completing Queen's Square, the Circus and the Royal Crescent in Bath (1728–1775), softened the monumental aspect of their architecture with vast green lawns.

Chiswick House (1725). This villa, repeating the theme of Palladio's Villa Capra, marks the triumph of neoclassicism in England after Wren's Baroque.

THE ART OF GARDENING IN THE 17TH AND 18TH CENTURIES

Gardening is a part of architecture in that it extends and complements the art of building.

French gardens. French Renaissance gardens were already laid out into orchards, walks and flower beds; and they contained latticework, pavilions and labyrinths.

At the start of the 17th century Claude Mollet created the first bordered flower beds. He was followed by André Le Nôtre, the father of so-called "French" gardens. Laid out along major axes like outdoor reception rooms, Le Nôtre's gardens made great use of water (in the form of pools, canals and waterfalls) as well as bordered flower beds and shrubbery planted and cut to form regular alleys. Le Nôtre shaped and controlled nature to follow the stately order and symmetry of classical construction.

Perhaps Le Nôtre's most glittering achievement—despite the splendidly composed gardens of Vaux-le-Vicomte—remains the beautiful park of Versailles. His ideas were mass-produced abroad, notably in palace gardens such as La Granja, Caserta, Sans-Souci, Peterhof and Schönbrunn.

Italian gardens. After awakening in the 16th century, Italian gardens hit their stride in the 17th. All sorts

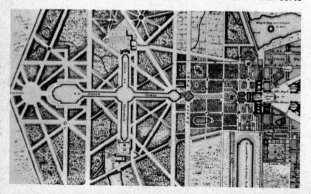

of vegetation were shaped, pruned and cut to form living statuary or architecture, and open-air theatres added a novel note to gardens of show places like the Garzoni, Gori and Marlia villas.

Lake Maggiore's Isola Bella (1670) was treated as an altar to the glory of nature. Its seven and a half acres, staggered on different levels, accentuate terraces, balustrades and stairways. The beauty of the site itself, the rare species planted and the skillfully laid out vistas of this masterful composition far outweigh the basic artificiality of the whole.

English gardens. The start of the 18th century saw the creation of an unheard-of type of garden which would eventually win out all over Europe: the English garden. Alexander Pope's garden in Twickenham is the loveliest

early example with its untrimmed trees, lack of symmetry and vast lawn running down to the river.

Other outstanding English gardens of this period were at Stowe, Chiswick, Castle Howard and Blenheim Palace. With the park at Stowe (1738), William Kent saw the charm of the irregular garden and thus invented English landscaping. Henceforth gardens consisted of spacious lawns planted with trees, surrounded by twisting alleys and occasionally containing whimsical outbuildings.

Around 1751, William Chambers popularised the Chinese garden built around a pagoda. This was later imitated at Chanteloup (p. 174) and Laeken and paved the way for Romanticism.

Gardens of Versailles (17th century). Designed by Le Nôtre along regular major axes, the gardens at Versailles epitomise French style, combining symmetry and balance.

Stowe Park (1738), the so-called Palladio bridge. This park was rearranged by William Kent who developed the idea of the irregular garden dotted with pseudo-antique structures.

EARLY TRENDS IN AMERICA

Most American construction in the 17th century reflects the architectural tastes of the colonisers. Thus the *colonial* style of wooden building based on neo-classicism reveals the Anglo-Saxon origins of this architecture. This neo-classical trend continued into the 18th century but with a slight French touch and a breath of Gothic. Benjamin Henry Latrobe (1764–1820) and Thomas Usteck Walter (1804–

1887) played important parts in building the Capitol in Washington, D.C., started in 1793. Its present dome, completed in 1865, spans more than 135 feet and, with the statue of Freedom at its summit, soars over 287 feet into the sky.

Few buildings of the first third of the 19th century showed much originality. Jefferson's University of Virginia (1817), Latrobe's Baltimore Cathedral (1818) and Walter's Girard College in Philadelphia (1847) all copied antique models, with little novelty added in spite of the high quality of plans made at the Beaux-Arts School of Paris. A Roman variation appeared in Boston in the form of Henry Hobson Richardson's Trinity Church.

NEO-CLASSICISM

Obviously neo-classicism has antique origins. The ruins of Herculaneum and Pompeii were still being acclaimed, and Percier and Fontaine had scoured Italy to fill their notebooks with careful inscriptions and renderings of Roman remains. In high favor was the Pompeian

Mount Vernon, Washington's home. Colonial style buildings using neo-Greek themes were still influenced by British architecture.

The White House, Washington, D.C. Built in 1792–1800 by James Hoban, burned by the British in 1814 and rebuilt by Hoban in 1815–1829, it illustrates in style the Greek revival so popular in the 19th century.

Paris: the Madeleine (1808–1842). This church, designed by Pierre-Alexandre Vignon, is a replica of a Greek temple, complete with sculpted pediment and colonnade.

style for which Queen Hortense's rooms in the Paris Hôtel de Beauharnais became so justly famous; and nudes and scenes from the distant past occupied most painters and sculptors.

Architects, on the other hand, though respectfully recording the forms and details of Greek, Roman and Egyptian remains, proclaimed their belief that beauty was essentially a matter of proportions. They believed in a plain and fundamental art, stripped of all superfluous ornament. Completely integrated with architecture, sculpture consisted of very shallow bas-reliefs on bare undecorated facades.

When Napoleon proclaimed the Empire and gave his civil servants such ancient titles as prefects, senators and tribunes, architecture followed suit in paying homage to the age of Augustus by erecting temples with quite varied purposes: stock exchange, theatre, church, museum, court, customs house or hospital. The Madeleine church and stock market were built in Paris as was the facade of the Palais Bourbon, now the National Assembly. Triumphal arches also followed the antique model: Chalgrin's Arc de Triomphe at the Etoile has four times the volume of its prototype, the Arch of Titus, while Percier and Fontaine copied the arches of Constantine and Septimus Severus in building their smaller but far more elegant arch of the Carrousel near the Louvre.

This trend continued as Napoleon's armies overran Europe, the far-flung results being, for example: in Berlin, Langhans' theatre and Brandenburg Gate; in Saint Petersburg, Ricard de Montferrand's Admiralty and

Leningrad: Saint Isaac's. Neoclassicism spread over Europe. Architecture everywhere repeated the same themes: pediments, colonnades and domes.

church of Saint Isaac and Thomas de Thornon's Stock Exchange; in Kazan, the church of Our Lady; and in Munich, the entrance of the sculpture gallery.

The reaction was not long in coming, and the painter Ingres became its spokesman: "Art is sick, and who will cure it? Will it die out completely? Yes, unless we choose another path: to study nature, as did the Greeks and Raphael." Whereupon artists began to re-examine the period extending from the 4th century to the Renaissance.

Architecture's return to the forms of the early Christian basilicas resulted in the construction of Paris' Nôtre-Dame de Lorette, the work of Lebas. The Quattrocento, the high Renaissance and the Arab-Norman polychrome decoration of Sicilian churches once again were all in high favor. A propensity for the rich and colorful Orient appeared in cafes by Hittorf along the Champs-Elysees, and in the church of Saint-Vincent-de-Paul which Hittorf did with Lepère.

At this very time, however, the painter Corot chose as his subjects the cathedrals of Chartres, Mantes and Sens, the Roman Forum and Italian gardens. The way to Romanticism, already indicated by English gardens, now lay wide open.

Berlin: the Brandenburg Gate, by K. G. Langhans. It has all the cold monumentality so typical of the neo-classic style.

the modern world | 5

After publication of Marc Antoine Laugier's *Essay on Architecture* (1752), and of the plans of Claude Nicolas Ledoux for the ideal city of Chaux (1773) and of his pupil Etienne Boullée for the spherical Newton cenotaph (1784), we could say that the direction of modern architecture had been fixed. Ledoux's director's house of Loue easily compares with Frank Lloyd Wright's famous "Fallingwater".

Though the French empire's neo-classicism had undoubtedly slowed down the modern movement, the seeds had nonetheless been planted, and all that the new forms needed in order to come into being were new materials.

Park Avenue at 47th Street, New York. Skyscrapers, the most spectacular expression of modern architecture, first appeared toward the turn of the century when steel frame construction became widespread.

These the 19th century provided—cast iron, iron, steel and later concrete—to make a totally different kind of architecture.

The advent of the 19th century brought strife and disorder in politics as well as in literature and the arts. Little by little, architects began to put more emphasis on techniques, to study geometry, the relationship of volumes, and the strength of materials—just at a time when past skills became known due to archeological discoveries in Babylonia, Assyria, China and Japan.

France still led Europe. Every artistic movement of the 19th century, from neo-classicism to Symbolism, originated in France, and its supremacy in the arts could be compared to Italy's during the Renaissance. Germany, Rumania, Belgium and Hungary all slavishly followed the trends in French art.

209

ROMANTICISM

Though the Romantic movement covered the years 1820 to 1850, it actually started to decline as early as 1830. Romanticism can be traced back to the beginning of the 18th century, to the French Regency period with its basic sensitivity and the admiration felt by architects of the time for Gothic art.

Sculpture and painting (biblical scenes, animals) were the first to be affected by this trend, whose conceptions diametrically opposed those of neo-classicism. Romanticism could not allow the necessity of ideal beauty or rigid drawing, preferring bright colors instead.

Again Gothic became the pet of architecture, with London's Westminster Palace (1840–1865), the work of Charles Barry and Augustus W. N. Pugin, being widely eulogized. Coinciding with the publication of Chateaubriand's *The Genius of Christianity* and Hugo's *Notre-Dame de Paris*, the movement gained fresh impetus from the newly established Historical Monuments Department. The city of Paris built the Gothic church of Sainte Clotilde, and houses everywhere flaunted such medieval ornaments as rosettes, spurs, gargoyles and Gothic arches. Furniture too followed the example set by architecture and the resulting style was called *troubadour*.

Completely eclectic, Romanticism did not depend merely on the Middle Ages for inspiration. Duban copiously applied Renaissance decoration to Paris' Beaux Arts School as well as to the Hôtel Pourtalès on the rue Tronchet. Lefuel, too, used

Renaissance ornamentation on the Flore and Marsan pavilions of the Louvre, whereas Vaudoyer drew on Vienna, Florence and the East for the cathedral of Marseille. For Paris' Sacré-Coeur, Abadie employed a weird combination of Romanesque elements from Saint Front in Périgueux and the cathedral of Angoulême. Soon afterward Romanticism degenerated into a hodgepodge of gingerbread.

A rather late contribution to the period, Charles Garnier's Paris Opéra (1862–1875), the Second Empire's major architectural product, also extended Romanticism. The basic plan of the opéra is both simple and sensible with excellent proportions. This carefully designed and completely functional theatre nobly fulfilled its purpose, which was not only to present theatrical performances but—perhaps of equal importance —to receive a large and glittering audience which included the emperor and empress. Garnier's flamboyantly rich decoration well reflects Napoleon III's regime. No pains were spared; it took 20 miles of plans to create the world's largest

Westminster Palace (1840–1865). A neo-Gothic structure by Charles Barry and Augustus Pugin, it illustrates the popularity of this style throughout Europe during the 19th century.

theatre (118,000 square feet). But what a difference between the overwhelming opulence of its grand staircase compared to the sobriety of the Louis XVI theatre in Bordeaux from which Garnier adopted the basic plan! Nevertheless, the Paris Opéra served as model for most theatres built in Europe during the 19th century, including Vienna's .Burgtheater (1874–1888).

The Romantic movement did not bypass Great Britain and Germany. Great Britain soon became covered with pseudo-medieval buildings including country houses and churches (All Saints, London, 1859). In any case, the *Gothic revival* has been practically continuous in England since the 18th century. When combined with the "picturesque", it resulted in such extravagant buildings as the Brighton Pavilion (1815–1820) built for the Prince of Wales by John Nash. Though its exterior reflects Moslem and Indian influences, metal columns predominate inside the building.

In Germany the neo-Gothic vogue expressed itself chiefly in buildings using brick architecture.

Paris: the Opéra (1862–1875). Charles Garnier's masterpiece is the most sumptuous expression of Second Empire architecture. Rising above the arcades, loggia, and attic is the profile of the dome.

REALISM AND THE TRIUMPH OF IRON

While painting evolved in a natural sequence from realism to naturalism and then to impressionism, architecture seemed to have arrived at its moment of truth. In his treatise on the subject, Durand wrote: "Architecture is above all building; forms are dictated by materials, economic factors and the client's needs." John Ruskin, in his *Seven Lamps of Architecture* (1849), proclaimed that the foremost quality of a building should be truth. A new ma-

Paris: the Eiffel Tower (1889). Built by Gustave Eiffel for the Universal Exposition of 1889, it is 984 feet high and rests on four pylons connected by purely decorative arches.

terial, iron, was to allow these principles to be translated into reality, and it became an instant success in France around 1840—over sixty years after the British had started using cast iron.

One of the first and most important structures to take

advantage of this modern, fireproof material was the Sainte-Geneviève Library (1843) in Paris. Within a quadrilateral of heavy masonry, the architect Henri Labrouste used iron to erect a light metal framework resting on extremely small points. This building, whose facade frankly reveals the interior arrangement, was the first to be specifically designed as a library, and as such was quickly imitated. Labrouste was also responsible for the interior arrangement of the Bibliothèque Nationale.

Iron's wonderful propensities made it possible with relatively small pillars to build astonishingly light spans over long distances. In a way this was a return—in a different material—to the medieval stone building techniques which Viollet-le-Duc had studied with such great thoroughness.

England's contribution to metal-framed architecture was the Crystal Palace (1851) built by Joseph Paxton in Hyde Park, London, to house the Great Exhibition.

Baltard adopted the same technique to cover Paris' vast Les Halles markets (1854–1866) and went on to use a metal framework for Saint-Augustin (1860–1871). Hittorf showed great daring in the huge spans of the Gare du Nord, another facade that clearly reflects its plan. The first prefabricated iron building was erected in Liverpool, England, by Peter Ellis (see Oriel Chambers, p. 8). Italy too plunged into the mainstream when Giuseppe Mengoni erected the gargantuan Victor Emmanuel Gallery in Milan (1865–1877).

Milan: the Victor Emmanuel Gallery (1865–1877). The work of Giuseppe Mengoni, this cruciform gallery has a large skylight supported by metal piers.

THE REVOLT AGAINST REALISM

Techniques kept evolving and the Paris Exposition of 1889 showed some of iron's infinite possibilities, with Eiffel's famous tower and Dutert and Contamine's Machinery Gallery, a vast hangar 1,390 feet long, 377 feet wide and 147 feet high.

Still another French initiative foretold the 20th century, for Vicat's advances in cement-making in the early 1820's inevitably led to the development of reinforced concrete. The first building using reinforced concrete was in Saint-Denis (1855) and the first building to make use of this material exclusively went up in 1892 at 1 rue Danton in Paris.

But toward the end of the century there was a turning away from realism and artless functionalism. After a few trials and errors a new art form was born about 1890—*Art Nouveau* (or as the French put it, *le style moderne*). This took its theme from nature, especially aquatic forms of life.

Curves and counter-curves made a comeback, facades swelled with strange tumor-like growths and stone

Barcelona: Casa de Mila (1905), by Antonio Gaudi, a masterpiece of Art Nouveau architecture. Its ornate facade masks a well-organized interior.

writhed and twisted into shapes having no functional purpose. Architecture became more the art of modeling than of construction.

As a result of the Paris Exposition of 1900, Art Nouveau became almost official and quickly won a coterie of enthusiasts in Germany, Belgium and, above all, Spain. In Barcelona Antonio Gaudi exploited his deep research into vegetable structure to create his own fantastic style. His church of Sagrada Familia (started in 1884 but unfinished) and apartment blocks display jutting forms, tilted columns and wavy roofs.

At the close of the century imaginative buildings appeared in many formerly tradition-bound cities. Horta's Tassel house (1893) and People's House (1898) in Brussels, Olbrich's Sezession gallery (1897) in Vienna and Mackintosh's Glasgow School of Fine Arts (1897–1907) all expressed this new kind of art, while Antonio Gaudi, its leading mentor, made the transition into the new century in 1905 with his Barcelona Casa de Mila. The coming century was to be characterised by the triumph of reinforced concrete and a struggle against academic rigidity.

19th CENTURY NORTH AMERICA

Louis Sullivan, alumnus of the Vaudremer studio in Paris and leader of the Chicago school, became the first of America's great modern architects. His Chicago Auditorium, one of the world's earliest multi-purpose buildings—simultaneously opera house, hotel and office building—cleared the way for modern architecture in the United States and launched the trend for towering sky-scrapers which steel construction had now made possible. As early as 1840 James Bogardus had pioneered in cast-iron framing, and in 1850 he built the first cast-iron building ever constructed in New York.

The first buildings to use visible framing were the Home Insurance Company building (1885) by William Le Baron Jenney and the Marquette building (1894) by John A. Holabird and Martin Roche, both in Chicago. The work of Daniel H. Burnham and John W. Root shows the important step which architects of that period took. Their Monadnock building in Chicago used masonry sustaining walls, while the Reliance building, erected at the same time, had a metal framework.

Sullivan's Wainwright Building in St. Louis (1890), Guaranty Building in Buffalo (1895) and the Carson, Pirie, Scott and Company department store in Chicago (1899) made the break with past architectural styles.

Canada. In the 17th century Canada built in the French manner, but later created a recognisable style of its own with Pierre Conefroy's church of Cap de la Madeleine (1715). Subsequently architecture came under British influence. The 19th century saw the imitation of older buildings, as witness Etienne Taché's Quebec Parliament.

Buffalo, Guaranty Building (1895). Louis Henri Sullivan, the first American architect to shake off the shackles of past traditions, showed here what could be done with metal framing.

Chicago: Carson, Pirie and Scott building (1899), another of Sullivan's works. Here the facade shows the lines of the metal framing and the openings consist of windows.

THE 20TH CENTURY AND THE BEGINNINGS OF MODERN ARCHITECTURE

Reinforced concrete architecture

Although reinforced concrete was invented in the 19th century, not until the 20th did new techniques develop in a plethora of original and daring forms.

In erecting the first reinforced concrete building on the rue Danton in Paris, François Hennebique and Edmond Arnaud had merely substituted concrete for stone. Its true vocation as framing and filler was yet to be discovered.

This step was taken by the Perret brothers in 1903 in their apartment building at 25 bis, rue Franklin, Paris (p. 9). The quite visible framework was considered near madness at this time, yet this supposed avante garde idea actually harked back to

---

Paris: Champs-Elysées Theatre (1913), by the Perret brothers, another example of early use of reinforced concrete. It has three superimposed auditoriums.

Notre-Dame de Royan, France (1960). Elevation and interior view of Guillaume Gillet's church. The V-shaped piers support a thin double-curved vault.

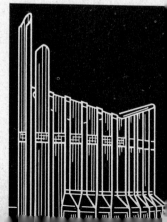

the Middle Ages when open bays predominated over solid structural elements. Far from resting on their laurels, the Perrets, in constructing the Ponthieu garage in 1905, went still further in the development of a structural system wherein concrete was limited to framing and walls were glass. Auguste Perret became the idolised French architect of the first half of the century.

The manifold variety of applications for reinforced concrete can be seen in Lecoeur's telephone office on the rue Bergère (1910) in Paris, Sauvage's building at 26 rue Vavin (1911), and the Perrets' theatre on the Champs-Elysées (1913); and also in Tony Garnier's stadium at Lyons (1916).

Nevertheless, reinforced concrete was taken up only by engineers and a handful of trend-setting architects like Le Corbusier. The ribbed dome conceived by architect Max Berg and engineer Trauer for Breslau's Centenary Hall (1913) anticipated Nervi's sports palace. In 1922 Eugène Freyssinet built a dirigible hangar at Orly whose parabolic shape was dictated wholly by technical considerations.

Now began a frantic competition to invent new forms. In Switzerland Robert Maillart invented the mushroom floor in Zurich. The Spaniard Eduardo Torreja created his trademark in the thin section roofing the Algeciras market (1933) and used as cantilever over the stands

at the Madrid racetrack (1935). Meanwhile, the Italian Pier Luigi Nervi proved himself the master of reinforced concrete with his very first building, the Florence stadium (1932). In France, Bernard Laffaille opened the way for prefabrication, and Sarger succeeded Laffaille in the work he had begun with Guillaume Gillet on the church at Royan.

Concrete architecture advanced another step with the application of pre-stressing (page 20), a technique generally attributed to Freyssinet.

A dynasty of Japanese architects—Mayekawa, Sakakura, Kikutake and, above all, Tangé—adapted concrete to their national traditions; and Le Corbusier's influence from this standpoint was considerable. Oscar Niemeyer, Lúcio Costa and Alfonso Reidy were making a name

New York: TWA terminal, Kennedy Airport (1956–1961), the last work of Eero Saarinen. Its 6,000-ton concrete roof rests on only four points.

for themselves in Brazil, and Niemeyer in particular found new uses for concrete at Pampulha and Brasília. The Mexican Candela's researches into hyperbolic paraboloids produced such spectacular triumphs as the Los Manantiales restaurant (1958).

In the United States Eero Saarinen and Louis Kahn, though moving in quite different directions, opened new vistas for contemporary architecture. Saarinen's use of free forms for the TWA terminal at New York's Kennedy Airport strikingly contrasts with the strict rigidity of Kahn's Richards Medical Research Center at the University of Pennsylvania. Despite fierce competition from steel, concrete always seemed to inspire new forms of expression, as demonstrated by Paul Rudolph's latest works and his school at Sarasota, Florida, in particular.

trends in contemporary architecture

Because of present-day architecture's bewildering diversity of styles, we have here tried to define the various trends by establishing the following categories:

The new neo-classicism developed by Auguste Perret finds expression in the use of concrete porticos and columns. He used concrete as early as 1899 in the casino at Saint-Malo, and his other early works in reinforced concrete include the rue Franklin apartment (1903) in Paris, the Champs-Elysées theatre (1913) and the church of Le Raincy (1922), one of the earliest churches to use this material.

Perret's later prolific work included the Casablanca docks, the church of Montmagny, the Grenoble observation tower, the concert hall of the National Music School, the National Warehouse, and the Public Works Museum in Paris and the postwar reconstruction of Le Havre. Today's young architects like to take their professional oaths in his apartment.

Cubist architecture: the Bauhaus school

This architecture, taught at the Bauhäuser of Weimar and Dessau between 1919 and 1933, was based on a synthesis of the plastic arts in an effort to create a new environment combined with the possibilities offered by industrial production. Concern for detail pushed the architects of this school to design everything down to furniture and even doorknobs. Its main protagonists were Walter Gropius and Marcel Breuer.

The first major work of German-born Gropius was the Alfeld factory complex of 1911 which featured a curtain wall of glass and steel. He followed this with a model factory for the Werkbund exposition of 1914 in Cologne. Windows rose from floor to ceiling and the staircase was enclosed in a glass cage.

Gropius designs for the Dessau Bauhaus (1926) called for studios, classrooms, exhibition galleries, student housing, a restaurant, an amphitheatre, a projection room and separate administration buildings.

As Gropius left the Bauhaus for Berlin in 1928 his place was taken by Breuer. Hitler forced Gropius to flee to England in 1934 and he then went to the United States in 1937 to become a professor at Harvard. Working with young members of the Architects' Collaborative, he built homes and schools like the Harvard Graduate Center in Boston (1950).

Of Hungarian origin, Marcel Breuer designed furniture before he replaced Gropius at the Bauhaus. He fled Berlin for London in 1935 and went on to America in 1937 where he joined Gropius until 1941. Since the war he has accomplished much, collaborating on Paris' UNESCO building and constructing the IBM research center at La Gaude near Nice (1961), as well as the Benedictine Saint John's Abbey near Collegeville, Minnesota.

Saint John's Abbey, Collegeville, Minnesota. A 1·11-foot reinforced concrete slab, resting on four supports, forms the bell tower of this Benedictine church, whose facade is one immense stained glass window.

The work of these two men is characterised by clean lines and the banishment of useless ornamentation.

Pure geometry and Mies van der Rohe

Also German-born, van der Rohe was the last director of the Bauhaus. He can be distinguished from his predecessors by his precision, his uncluttered asceticism, his striving for utter purity of line and his almost exclusive use of steel and glass.

Even at the beginning of his career his work was avant-garde, one of his most typical buildings being the German pavilion for the 1929 Barcelona Exhibition. It contained absolutely nothing, as if itself alone was to be Germany's contribution.

To escape the Nazi menace, van der Rohe emigrated to the U.S. in 1937 and became head of the Architectural School of the Illinois Institute of Technology.

With a floor raised above ground level, steel framing and long glass panels, the Farnsworth house in Plano, Illinois (1950), perfectly illustrates van der Rohe's architectural concepts. The house is entirely transparent except for an inner utilitarian core. Other triumphs include the 25-story apartment

Chicago: Mies van de Rohe's two great 25-story apartment units along Lake Shore Drive (1951). Their aesthetic effect relies on harmonious proportions and the appearance of the structural elements.

skyscrapers on Chicago's Lake Shore Drive (1951), four 28-story skyscrapers on Commonwealth Promenade overlooking Lake Michigan (1957), two skyscrapers at 900 Esplanade in Chicago, and New York's Seagram building, with 38 floors, which he designed in collaboration with Philip Johnson in 1958.

Frank Lloyd Wright and "organic architecture"

Wright was the first epoch-making architect of the 20th century. Starting out with individual homes, he went on to much larger buildings and introduced many startling innovations in his "organic architecture," designed to harmonize buildings with their users and surroundings.

Proving his talent with the daring Larkin Building of 1904 in Buffalo (completely enclosed and air-conditioned, with built-in furniture), he then switched to steel and a more open plan for his Robie House of 1909.

His most characteristic work is his own home of Taliesen in Spring Green, Wisconsin, built of local stone and weathered wood. Later he made architectural history with Tokyo's Teikoku, or Imperial Hotel, which, thanks to his foresighted design, easily withstood the terrible earthquake of 1923. Subsequently he worked on Taliesen West, his winter home near Phoenix, Arizona, where he built a school for his apprentices, incorporating his basic principles of horizontality that blends with natural settings.

"Fallingwater," his fabled villa cantilevered over a stream in Bear Run, Pennsylvania, dates from 1936 and this was followed by even more daring projects: the Johnson Wax Company administration buildings and laboratory tower in Racine, Wisconsin (1936–1939); New York's spiral-shaped Guggenheim Museum (1956–1959); his theatre at Dallas (1960).

"Fallingwater," Bear Run, Pennsylvania (1936). Frank Lloyd Wright's celebrated house shows his wish to integrate architecture with landscape.

The functional architecture of Le Corbusier

Le Corbusier's written works carry nearly as much weight as his buildings, and his *Toward an Architecture* (1923) had a lasting impact on the younger generation. This book came on the heels of a city-planning project for a city of three million which he had presented at the Salon d'Automne in 1922.

For the International Decorative Arts Exposition in 1925 he built the Esprit Nouveau pavilion which caused a sensation. Five years later he designed Radiant City, a multi-dwelling complex in a single building, but its fruition was long delayed. His entire aim was to reconcile aesthetic with functional requirements.

In France he built "radiant cities" for Marseilles, Rézé, and Briey, the Swiss and

Ronchamp: Notre-Dame-du-Haut (1950–1954), Le Corbusier's masterpiece. The thin shell of the roof accentuates the curved lines of the church, in which there is not one straight line or right angle.

Brazilian pavilions of the University of Paris' student housing complex, the pilgrims' church of Ronchamp (1950–1954) and the Tourette convent (1955–1959).

Elsewhere, he was responsible for the Carpentier Institute of Plastic Arts at Harvard, the Rio de Janeiro University building, the city planning project for Bogotá, Colombia, the administrative centre of Chandigarh in India, the Tokyo Museum, a "radiant city" in Berlin and the Philips Pavilion at the Brussels World's Fair.

Le Corbusier was the unflagging foe of academic

thinking, government-controlled education and senseless city planning, and he never ceased to crusade for the qualities of naturalism and light so evident in his buildings.

Oscar Niemeyer
and the search for new forms
Ex-pupil of le Corbusier and creator of Brasília, Oscar Niemeyer underwent a spell of unashamed gigantism in Rio de Janeiro before he constructed Brazil's new capital.

Sao Paulo's Modern Art Week in 1922 deeply impressed the young Niemeyer. On obtaining his degree in 1934 he went to work for Lúcio Costa, a great fan of Le Corbusier. Together, they built Rio de Janeiro's Education and Health Ministry from designs supervised by Le Corbusier.

Niemeyer's first project in his own right was the nursery school of the Obra de Berco foundation (1938), and his

---

Milan: the Pirelli Tower (1959). The work of Pier Luigi Nervi and Gio Ponti, this unusual triangular-section tower diminishes as it rises.

Brasília: the cathedral (1959). Oscar Niemeyer's church, 230 feet in diameter, can hold 4,000 worshippers. The structure rests on 21 concrete supporting elements.

talent was further confirmed by the resort complex in Pampulha which he was asked to design by the city's mayor, Kubitschek.

The fresh style of his Pampulha church, Saint Francis of Assisi—which could reasonably be called Modern Baroque—created a great stir. His Boavista Bank Building in Rio de Janeiro, on the other hand, was rigorously functional with piles, curtain walls and protection against the tropical sun.

From 1950 the scope of Niemeyer's vision grew by leaps and bounds. In Petropolis he built the Hotel Quitandinha, a 33-story structure with 5,700 rooms and two hundred shops; and in Belo Horizonte the enormous Kubitschek housing development where elevated buildings rest on V-shaped pillars. This trend culminated in his designs for Brasília, which included the Aurora Palace, the National Congress Palace and the cathedral with its diameter of 230 feet and 4,000-seat capacity.

Because of its Baroque freeform building, set in Burle Marx's fanciful tropical gardens, Brazilian architecture of the 1950's has captured the imagination of the world.

Pier Luigi Nervi and functional beauty

Intrigued by structural theory, Pier Luigi Nervi completely revamped concrete construction techniques and moved them away from traditional forms. His first important work was the Florence stadium (1932), followed by aircraft hangars at Orbetello, Orvieto and Torre del Lago (1936–1941). With prefabricated elements resting on inclined, anti-stress pillars these hangars opened new horizons for reinforced concrete.

Nervi's wholly functional yet beautiful works proved that an industrial aesthetic could exist. Turin's Exposition Hall (1949), Bologna's tobacco factory (1952) and the Gatti spinning mill in Rome (1953) amply prove this.

Nervi's genius soars to its greatest heights where large spans are required: the festival hall of the Nuove Terne in Chianciano (1952), the UNESCO conference hall in Paris (1957), the Flaminio stadium (1958) and the Sports Palace in Rome (1957).

Though spans have been a Nervi specialty, his skill in building upward was demonstrated with the Pirelli Tower in Milan (1959), built with Gio Ponti. It has since become an architectural landmark.

Neo-Baroque. At the turn of the century Gaudi created a vogue for neo-Baroque, and Wright could be said to be Baroque in such buildings as the Guggenheim Museum. Niemeyer goes quite Baroque at Pampulha, particularly with his restaurant which follows the contours of the lake, and Candela's saddleback roofs are nothing if not Baroque. Le Corbusier, too, sets a fine swashbuckling example in his chapel of Ronchamp.

Even so, the most incredible architect in this field was Finnish-born Eero Saarinen, son of Eliel Saarinen, himself a second-prize winner in the competition for the Chicago Tribune Tower. Eero Saarinen settled in the United States and died there prematurely in 1961. Divorcing himself completely from the Scandinavian tradition and momentarily influenced by Mies van der Rohe, Saarinen launched a series of highly individual designs, of which the first flowering was the General Motors Technical Center in Detroit. Called the American Versailles, this building, which ranks as one of the seven wonders of U.S. architecture, established once and for all a high standard for industrial design.

Yale University, New Haven, Conn. For the roof of the Ingalls hockey rink, Saarinen used a flexible covering supported by a mesh of steel cables.

Saarinen's true personality blossomed after 1950 in such buildings as the Ingalls hockey and skating rinks for Yale University, the TWA terminal at New York's Kennedy Airport and the terminal of Washington's Dulles Airport. His work is anything but standardised. In fact, its very diversity tends to prove that for each project a form must be found to fit the function.

The Scandinavian influence.
Two Finnish disciples of Le Corbusier made rewarding contributions to modern architecture. The first was Alvar Aalto, creator of the Paimio sanatarium (1929) and the Viipuri library; and Erik Bryggman, responsible for the Lutheran funeral chapel at Turku. Finland may also be proud of its native son Viljo Revell, who won out over five hundred other architects for the commission to build Toronto's new city hall.

In the field of public housing the satellite towns which have mushroomed up around Helsinki and Stockholm soon acquired reputations as models of their kind. Perhaps Tapiola (1951–1965) gained the most renown through its exceptional site, excellent design and reasonable density.

Alvar Aalto's work packs universal appeal. His first great success, the Paimio sanitarium, raised a storm of controversy at the International Architects' Convention (C.I.A.M.) held in Athens during 1933. His Sulina pulp factory exemplified his understanding of human requirements while his Helsinki Pensions Office differs pleasingly from the endless stacked offices common to most administrative buildings.

Aalto could have stayed in the United States, like many of his European colleagues who found refuge there, but he preferred to return to Finland to help in the reconstruction of his own country.

Tapiola, Finland (aerial view), a remarkably successful example of city planning in which architecture blends perfectly with landscape. Most of the buildings are of local materials and are low in outline.

private housing

Reams are written about major buildings but precious little about individual homes. Yet the world's great architects have never neglected this field. Perret's villa in Garches, Wright's fabulous "Fallingwater" house and his low horizontal "prairie houses" with vast living rooms and overhanging roofs, Le Corbusier's Savoye villa in Poissy (1929), Mies van der Rohe's Farnsworth house, Breuer's Harnischmachers House in Wiesbaden and Aalto's villa Mairea near Noormark all exemplify this. Some architects have even made this field their major concern, among them the Australian Harry Seidler and, above all, Vienna-born Rich-

Sorrel House, California. Like all Richard Neutra's houses, it fits perfectly into landscape, dramatising the contrast between its simple forms and rich materials.

ard Neutra, who settled in the United States in 1923.

The latter, influenced by the Bauhaus, Wright and Japanese construction, became an authority on residential construction in California. The beauty of his own work depends on the juxtaposition of simple, pure volumes, contrasting with rich materials chosen at the site. His houses merged into the landscape, but nature is also made an integral part of the house via glass walls and open air extensions. His Moore, Sorrell and Hansch houses are well-known examples.

CITY PLANNING

While the term city planning is of recent date, the art or science that it describes is as old as cities themselves. Applied first to a city and its immediate surroundings, it becomes regional development when expanded to include a particular area, a country or a group of countries. Greek and Roman towns were laid out according to pre-established plans, and the great cities of France sprang up over the sites of Gallo-Roman cities where major arteries, the *cardus* and *decumanus*, crossed at right angles.

Cities in the Middle Ages were formed or grew according to two different plans. Either they were concentric, in which case blocks of houses radiated out from the church; or they were checkerboard so that straight parallel streets intersected at right angles.

From the 6th to the 16th century, cities often were enclosed in networks of walls and fortifications and their character thus depended on the site (as at Carcassonne).

Bram, France, is typical of concentric medieval cities in which blocks of houses radiate outward from a central church.

In China during the same period, walls were added in series as they became necessary.

During the 17th and 18th centuries, the cities overflowed their ramparts, which had in any case become useless except perhaps for some of Vauban's new fortified towns. Now came new settings of colonnades and royal squares whose inspiration was monumental perspective. Louis XIV launched the idea of a subsidiary capital and Ledoux drew up plans for a Utopian metropolis.

Reconstruction always becomes necessary after wars, and people suddenly become aware of the meaning of city planning. With suburbs proliferating and private homes going up haphazardly, the need for city planning—over a certain section or over a whole city—is obvious.

After World War I the Siegfried-Carnudet law required all French cities of over ten thousand inhabitants, as well as all hard-hit cities, to have a development plan specifying aesthetic and hygienic restrictions. These called for limiting building heights, making green spaces mandatory and regulating water distribution, drainage and sewer networks. Garden cities were also planned in France. Krupp's German *Siedlungen* (settlements; 1906) had foreshadowed the trend, which was further developed by the Englishman Ebenezer Howard (1918) in his rural New Towns, limited to 32,000 inhabitants. The United States embraced the concept, naturally on a far vaster scale; the city of Gary, about 25 miles from Chicago, now numbers around 178,000 inhabitants. Whole quarters were developed and residential units built as such.

Today entire cities are

Plan of Peking. As the city overran its southern ramparts, an additional wall was built around the new section in the 16th century.

New York: a cluster of skyscrapers.
Typically American, skyscrapers are built mainly for economic reasons—to get maximum useful surface from a limited site.

Bobigny-les-Courtillières, France.
This serpentine building forms part of one of the new towns built to relieve France's population expansion.

planned and built as a unit. Thus an architect who began his career designing individual dwellings may eventually have to plan entire cities, as did Le Corbusier at Chandigarh, Yet city planning must never overlook the past. While it may appear simple to plan a new city, respecting the different human functions as defined in the Athens Charter (1943)—to live, to work, to relax and to circulate—the problem becomes infinitely more complex when it is a question of streamlining old cities or even extending them beyond their boundaries.

The population explosion means that developing or merely enlarging existing cities no longer suffices. After an initial attempt to solve the housing problem by groups of dwellings (as at Sotteville-lès-Rouen) or a single large building (Le Corbusier's "radiant cities"), satellite towns or "large complexes" for 30,000 inhabitants had to be constructed around the old cities.

At first these large developments were criticized for their uniformity and lack of adequate facilities. Later, though, emulating the Scandinavians and British, they acquired satisfactory road systems, commercial centres and facilities for youth, culture and recreation.

Nevertheless, these developments are still dismissed as being nothing more than "dormitory towns", and it is now evident that the ideal formula is to create autonomous population units, complete with occupational outlets for the people which will keep them on the spot. This requires industry (but clean atomic-powered industry) and, above all, vast green spaces and a communications network designed so that pedestrians can be kept separate from motor traffic. Tapiola in Finland and Farsta in Sweden both well exemplify this type of development. Much good work is being done along these lines each year at the same time that enormous sums are being spent to rehabilitate old urban centres and poorly organised suburbs where buildings have been allowed to mushroom indiscriminately. The planned development of Paris's Défense quarter, with the fabulous C.N.I.T. exhibition hall as its centre, has quite revolutionised the city's western suburbs.

Considerable city planning

is going on everywhere. Newly discovered riches (natural gas, uranium, petroleum), the popularisation of winter sports, the development of heretofore isolated coastal areas and recovering land from the sea (as in Tokyo, where Tangé has designed a city built entirely on piles) are all opportunities for projects wherein both man and nature can be respected.

the future of architecture

The future of architecture will depend on how much importance city planning allows it. Solitary works by individual architects have had their day. Henceforth archi-tecture will be a collective art; the product of a team operating within a city planning project.

A new Baroque had appeared in reaction against the rigid verticals and horizontals of the Cubist tendency, and Saarinen's TWA Terminal in New York has opened new and unlimited horizons, thanks to techniques using pre-stressed concrete, steel, light alloys, plastics and glass which also is now pre-stressed.

The architecture of the latter half of the 20th century falls within the realm of research. There is talk of cities in space, underground developments and even the immateriality of structures.

Notwithstanding, architecture will remain an art even in an era of prefabrication and industrialisation, and there will always be architects to stamp it with their genius.

Model of a development project for the Defense quarter of Paris. Skyscrapers form an integral part of a city planning scheme which will change the face of an entire district.

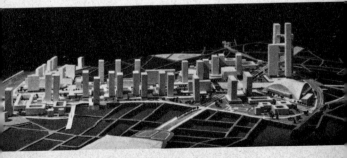

INDEX

Bold-face figures indicate illustrations.

ABCDEF